BLACK COUNTRY
Memories

Black Country Memories

I dedicate this to the people of the Black Country who have kept alive our dialect and whose hard work was vital in making England the greatest manufacturing nation in the world.

BLACK COUNTRY
Memories

CARL CHINN

BREWIN BOOKS

First published by
Brewin Books Ltd, 56 Alcester Road,
Studley, Warwickshire B80 7LG in 2004
www.brewinbooks.com

Reprinted November 2004
Reprinted February 2007
Reprinted November 2011

ISBN: 978-1-85858-266-5

A Cataloguing in Publication Record
for this title is available from the British Library.

Typeset in Times
Printed in Great Britain by
Berforts Group Limited.

CONTENTS

ACKNOWLEDGEMENTS

It is a thrill to be writing a local history feature for the *Express and Star*. The paper is not only the biggest-selling evening newspaper in the country outside London, but also it is marked out by its commitment to its region and the people of that region. There can be few papers that are as local as the *Express and Star* and that commitment to localness affects positively every aspect of its reporting and coverage. The Black Country is fortunate to have a paper so dedicated to the well being of Black Country folk. I thank the editor of the *Express and Star*, Adrian Faber, and its management for giving me the opportunity to write so extensively about the Black Country. Adrian has been a constant source of support and encouragement to me and like me is a proud West Midlander. My appreciation is also due to Charlie Moss, Adrian's secretary, who carefully and thoughtfully collects all the memories and photos sent in to me; Graeme Andrew, the news sub-editor, who puts together my pages in such a talented and sensitive way; and Mark Green, internet information control officer, who has played an important role in sourcing photographs. I also thank the readers of the *Express and Star* who have honoured me by sharing with me their memories and letting me see their photos and precious memorabilia.

Chapter 1

THE TIPTON SLASHER

Fighter who survived taking it on the Chinn

When I was a kid I never knew my Grandad Perry to walk. Grandad had been struck down by multiple sclerosis when he was in his forties and about the last time he wasn't in a wheelchair was when he walked Our Mom down the aisle in 1954.

But even though he couldn't get about, Our Grandad was one of the most important people in our lives. On a Sunday everyone in the family seemed to meet at Our Mom's and after a couple of tots of whiskey, Our Grandad would raise the one arm he could move and beckon me and Our Kid to him. Looking back, we must have been eight or nine when Grandad's words began to make a mark upon us.

'Don't you two ever forget, ma lads', he'd urge. 'What's that, Grandad?'

'Don't you two ever forget, you're related to the Tipton Slasher.' Now, this wasn't something we went around bragging about. Coming from the south east side of Brummagem, we knew about the Black Country and that Tipton was in it and that was about it. And we'd also heard about Jack the Ripper and so in our childish minds we thought we'd got someone in our family who went around some place called Tipton slashing people with a knife.

For years Our Grandad impressed upon us the need to be proud of our relationship to the Tipton Slasher but we didn't take much notice until just before Grandad died. It was his last Christmas with us, although we didn't know that. I was sixteen and Our Darryl was just fifteen. We'd gone up town to Birmingham city centre to buy presents, and as we always did when we were up town we went to Hudson's bookshop. It was a magical

Carl in his office, at his home in Birmingham, with the book he found at Hudson's bookshop which set him on the quest to find out more about his famous Black Country relative.

place, like an Aladdin's Cave with little rooms above and below ground, filled with shelves stacked with the treasure of books of all kinds. Suddenly it was as if one book jumped out to us and leaped into our hands. It was called *The Tipton Slasher* and was by Tom Langley. It was the winter of 1972, just a year or so after decimalisation, and the price on the book was still five shillings.

Me and Our Kid couldn't catch our breath. There was a Tipton Slasher. It wasn't just a story made up by Our Grandad and this relation was important enough to have been written about.

We grabbed hold of the book and bought it without looking at it. When we got home we couldn't wait to tell Our Mom and her sister, Our Lynne. We all sat down and as fast as we could we rushed through it to find out about the Tipton Slasher.

Carl's Grandad, Arthur Perry, whose grandfather, William, was the nephew of the Tipton Slasher.

Now as any Black Country chap and wench could tell you, the Tipton Slasher was one of the greatest of all bare-fisted boxing champions of England. He got his name because he came from Tipton and he slashed with his right hook, but his real name was Bill Perry. Dead excited, we thought 'he's got the same surname as Our Grandad'. So without telling Grandad we'd got the book we started to quiz him about what he knew about his people. All Grandad could tell us was that his own father was a Thomas Perry, who was a Black Country man who'd been a drummer boy in the Boer War and who'd come to Brum as a young man. Grandad knew little more bar that his own grandfather was a William Perry and that he'd been named after his uncle, Bill Perry the famed Tipton Slasher.

So what we did then was to write to Mr Langley, telling him what little we had pulled together and asking him if he could confirm that Our Grandad was related to the Tipton Slasher. Mr Langley must have been a kind man to get back to a pair of Brummagem lads who daynt know A from a bull's foot. But get back he did. He'd got in touch with a very old lady who was a niece or great niece of the Tipton Slasher and she confirmed that she'd had a cousin called William. Any road up, we wrapped up the book for Grandad for Christmas, along with Mr Langley's letter. We had to open the present for Grandad as he could hardly move his arms by now and we had to let him know what it was as his eyes were failing.

When he heard it was a book on the Tipton Slasher it was as if a sparkler had lit up his face. Our Grandad was in his oiltot. Everything he'd passed on to us was vindicated. Grandad never swore, but all he did say was 'God blige me. I told y'

Seen in 1972, this was the burial place of the Tipton Slasher in Saint John's Churchyard, Kates Hill, Dudley. According to a news story of the time, people were travelling from far and wide to see William Perry's resting place. The inscription reads, "William Perry (known as the Tipton Slasher), born 1820, died 1880. Champion of England 1850-57. The memorial was erected by public subscription, October 1926." In 1950 local people failed in an appeal to put a monument on the grave.

dayn I. I told y' we was related to the Tipton Slasher.' Our Grandad died that February coming. When Our Mom opened up his little purse after he'd gone there was just a few coins in it. Amongst them were two florins. Our Kid and me had one each. Mine is by me now as I write this.

Our Grandad had no money to leave us. He had no property to will us, nor had he jewels or fine things for us to inherit. But if Our Grandad had nothing material to give us he left us things much more worthy. He left us his example of good humour and bravery in never bowing down to a vile illness. He left us his words, the words of a West Midlander who ate pieces when he was clammed, who proudly called his daughters 'Ma wench', who chucked his rubbish in miskins and who'd known what it was to collar every day for little reward. And he left us his stories.

The famous painting of the Tipton Slasher at the High Street, Tipton premises of the Tipton and Coseley Building Society in 1979. Left to right are Stuart Eaton, Edwin Holden and Edwin Holden.

Stuart J. Eaton was interested to see in 'Black Country Memories' this photo of him standing to the left of Edwin Holden and Tom Fisher and he has written to me with more information about the purchase of the portrait of William Perry by Tipton and Coseley Building Society. At the time Stuart was Chief Executive of the Society and when he finally resigned from the board on 31 December 1997 he had worked for 56 years for the same organisation. Stuart tells me that "Tom Fisher, a Director, brought to the Board's attention that the portrait was being sold by auction at a hotel in Knowle, and he and I were duly authorised to go and bid within a limited amount.

"I understand that it had remained hidden behind some wardrobe at a property in Willenhall and was not in a very good condition. We were successful and made arrangements for the picture and the frame to receive restorative attention.

"The frame was done by one Leonard Chalstrey, a retired schoolmaster, who taught at both Princes End and Willingsworth schools and was a master craftsman at any type of woodworking, in particular carving. A few years ago his elder son, John (now Sir John) was Lord Mayor of London. Unfortunately Leonard was unable to attend when the photograph was taken, but Edwin Holden was there as Chairman at that time."

Through that story of the Tipton Slasher, me and Our Kid were being bonded – without us noticing it – with our people who had gone before. We were coming to recognise that we were not on our own, that we were part of those whom we had never known but who had helped make us. And we were becoming alert to the importance of that link with the past that means that we owe a duty not only to those yet to come but to those who have gone. I know this. I am proud to be the grandson of Arthur Perry and through him I am proud to have the blood of a proper Black Country mon, Bill Perry The Tipton Slasher.

A Legend Who Beat 'Em All and Never Gave Up

They did things their own way in Gornal – even fighting was according to Gornal Rules and not prize fighting regulations, as young Bill Perry learned when he was challenged by Skim Skimmy. Skim was a massive chap and he was fixed upon taking on the Tipton lad whose scrapping prowess was the talk of the Black Country.

They would battle it out for a donkey and a bag of sand, although both men also betted all the money they could scrape together on their own victory. The two of them would fight in bare feet in a match that had no rounds and which ended only when one of them was knocked out, disqualified or cried "Enough!" Anything went, bar for kicking and gauging.

Hundreds turned out that day early in 1837 when Skim Skimmy the pride of Gornal and Bill Perry the cock of Tipton met on the side of the cut at Park Hall in Walsall. The first blows were struck at two in the afternoon and three hours later as darkness overwhelmed the light they were still at it. With the fight undecided, Skim and Bill set to again the next day. The rain pelted down and the story is told that Perry, with the typical dry humour of a proper Black Country mon, was lying on top of the Gornal bloke when he became fed up of belting his opponent. "Ave yoh ad

When the Tipton Slasher lost it all from the television drama, 'Gie it some Ommer'. The Tipton Slasher, played by Pat Roach, fights Little Tom Sayers, played by Gordon Corbett. Sayers won the contest. Ray Hingley is in the centre.

enuff?" asked Bill. "No, I ay", Skim threw back defiantly. "Well, yoh con cum on top fer a change, Ar'm getting wet through up ere", flung back Bill. After two hours Skimmer was laid out and a hardly marked Perry was announced the winner. Winning a pony, £25, on bets and selling the donkey and sand at the side of the ring, Bill Perry headed back to celebrate with his pals in his headquarters at the 'Fountain Inn', Tipton.

Born in 1819, Bill belonged to a family of boatees, living and working on and alongside the cut. Like all poor youngsters, Bill had to play his part in pulling in the money that kept the family independent and out of the hated workhouse. Aged seven he joined his old mon in taking night soil from Tipton into the countryside of South Staffordshire. It was a dirty, stinking and vile job fetching away the mess of cess pits and closets, but poor families like the Perrys had no choice. They had to collar or be clammed. Hungry days there were, and days a many without the proper food – so much so that Bill was ravaged by rickets, the deficiency of Vitamin D that softens the bones. This bent young Perry's left leg so much that its pronounced angle led him to be known as K Legs.

With a disability and lacking learning through no schooling, still Bill Perry stood out. A giant of a lad, begenst he was twelve he was tipping six feet tall and for all his youth he was feared amongst the boatees as a hard and relentless fighter who knew not what it was to back down. It wasn't long before Bill's fame burst out of his home town of Tipton. At the age of sixteen he was grafting as a navvy in London where he had his first prize fight. He took on a heavier, older and more experienced Irishman called Barnet Dogherty and bested him. A pugilistic reporter declared that Perry's "shoulders are truly tremendous and there are great pads of muscle on his upper arms so that his width is enhanced. This handsome kindly looking fellow is a sculptor's model from the waist up, but his knees are knocked to a remarkable degree."

The wraps officially came off a £25,000 statue of Tipton's most famous son, with Sandwell Mayor, John Sullivan, doing the honours back in May 1993. The statue is situated in Coronation Gardens, Tipton, and is mounted on a brick plinth overlooking the 'Fountain Inn'.

A year later, Bill Perry was back in Tipton and in 1836 he took on Ben Spilsbury of Brummagem. It was in this fight that the Black Country fighter gained his nickname of the Tipton Slasher, for he hammered the Brummie with round right-arm blows in a slashing motion – so powerfully indeed that he bosted Ben's jaw and several of his ribs. It was soon after this fight that Bill Perry beat Skim Skimmy. The men of Gornal were not best pleased at their loss and they fetched their champion, Jem Scummer, to sort out the Tiptonian Hercules. The pair came to blows just before Christmas 1837 in a field close to Gornal Wood. Eighteen years old, Bill was now six feet one and a half tall and fourteen stone in weight. After an inconclusive few rounds on 22 December, they met again the next day. In the 31st round the Gornal man was laid out and the Tipton Slasher was £25 the richer.

Tough, afeared of no-one and galvanised by years of hardship, yet Bill Perry was not a vicious man and nor was he one without sensitivity. In the late 1830s he met the love of his early life, Jane Cotterill. Jane come out of Old Cross Street, Tipton and was a pit bonk wench. Her family were devout Prims, Primitive Methodists, and her teetotaller father railed against blood sports of all kinds. The pugilistic and heavy drinking Bill must have appeared the antithesis of all that old man Cotterill believed in, but still the courtship grew. Each Sunday Bill would walk Jane to a little chapel by Walker Street and afterwards they would sit and chat in the cemetery. But Bill's heart was bosted when Jane was taken by smallpox in 1839. At her funeral this big man blarted his eyes up, and till the day he died his favourite song would be 'My pretty Jane, why do you look so sad'.

By now the Tipton Slasher was managed by a crafty chap from Birmingham called Johnny Broome who knew the Black Country scrapper had to go to London to really make his name. This he did. He challenged all the best fighters in England to take him on. Few dared. Ben Caunt, Jem Bendigo, Deaf Burke and others – all celebrated for their strength, ability and power and all assiduously avoided the Tipton Slasher. Making money from exhibitions and from the cash put up by opponents who failed to turn up in the ring, still Bill Perry wanted the accolade of uncontested champion of England. At last one man took up his challenge. It was another West Midlander, Tass Parker of West Bromwich. After two fights in 1843 in which the skilful Tass strove to avoid physical contact with Bill, the Tiptonian knocked out his protagonist in their third encounter three years later.

Then in December 1850, the Slasher beat Tom Paddock of Redditch for the championship. Bill Perry challenged the great Jem Bendigo to hand over his championship belt or meet him in the ring. Bendigo did neither. Years later, Bendigo was converted and on one occasion preached at a revivalist meeting in the Black Country. His avoidance of the Tipton Slasher had not been forgotten, for as he pronounced to the crowd that he was there to fight the Devil, a Black Country chap shouted out, "Ar, an if yoh dodge im like yoh dodged the Slasher e won't stand much chance!"

Losing the championship in 1851when he was deemed to foul Harry Broome of Birmingham, Bill regained it quickly when Broome forfeited a second match. No-one would now enter into the ring with the pride of Tipton and hailed as the champion prize fighter of England, he retired to keep the 'Champion of England' beer house in Spon Lane, West Bromwich. With his wife and sister minding the pub, the Tipton Slasher was feted across the land, but there was something that niggled Bill Perry – the words of the Dudley Devil. The last of the Black Country cunning men, Elijah Dunn saw the future and told fortunes. When Bill Perry went to see him he was warned:

Slasher, yoh'll stop as yoh started.
Yoh'll get all yoh gid in one goo.
Yoh and yoer pub will be parted,
Tom Little will mek it come true.

The Dudley Devil's warning went unheeded.

In 1857 Tom Sayers challenged the Tipton Slasher for the championship. Bill was 38, sixteen stone and badly out of shape through boozing and good living but he decided to risk everything against little Tom Sayers, a middleweight who was just eleven stone and five feet eight tall. Selling his pub, furniture, trophies, watches and anything else of value, he staked the lot on beating little Tom. The fight took place on 16 June 1857. Early on the Slasher was shattered by a terrible blow to the temple and all his craft was punched from him. He was cut to pieces by the smaller yet fitter and leaner man, but still the Slasher would not ask for barley. For one hour and forty-two minutes he was punished by Sayers. At last, the Slasher's backers stopped the fight but the game Tiptonian still would not say 'Enough'. Blinded by his own blood, he had to be held down by his four seconds whilst the sponge was thrown in.

Skint, Bill Perry returned to the boats and shifting night soil. The warning of the Dudley Devil had come true. He stopped as he started. He had got all he'd gid in one goo, for unmarked as he was from years of beating others he was scarred horribly in one fight. He and his pub had been parted. And Tom Little had made it come true.

But the Slasher was not broken. His mind and body injured badly, even so he worked hard and eventually bought his own house in Gibbett Lane, Bilston. A good husband and father, Bill Perry died on Christmas Eve 1880 in his own home. He was the last of his kind:

And Perry bold of Tipton town, all bone and muscled meat,
Who smiling comes up to the scratch on firmly planted feet,
And moving forwards fights and fights and cannot brook retreat,
When he is gone the Prize Ring goes 'twill die in his defeat.
The last old English pugilist,
One of the olden time.
(From the 'Fine Old English Pugilist').

Bill Perry was a hard man in a hard age, but his heart was never hardened and nor was his soul. He never knew what it was to give in, he never cheated and he never forgot where he came from. He is a man of whom the Black Country is rightly proud. The undaunted Bill Perry, the Tipton Slasher.

The Tipton Slasher was said to have sparred with a huge ape and sometimes a bear. When the house in which he lived was knocked down, a stuffed ape was found in the attic, which is believed to have been kept as a pet by Bill Perry. In 1949, the ape was adorning the bar of a Horseley Heath pub.

Peter Dryburgh, senior support worker at William Perry Court, Shakespeare Road Tipton, has kindly sent me some newspaper cuttings that they keep at this Trident housing project. One of them includes the memories of Mrs Mary Cotton and tells of the fate of the ape, Bill Perry's sparring partner. Mary still had in her possession the bible of Timothy, the famed pugilist's brother, in which were details of the family tree, and she contacted the Tipton Civic Society in 1992 when it was involved in the campaign to erect a statue to honour Bill Perry the Tipton Slasher in the town of his birth. She confirmed that the fighter did spar with the ape, which was killed during one such training session at the 'Three Horse Shoes' pub in Ocker Hill Road, which was run by the Slasher's nephew, William.

According to Mary, "Apparently one day the ape was playing up and bit the Slasher on the hand. He punched it and it fell down a flight of steps into the cellar, stone dead. William Perry Junior stuffed the ape and mounted it in a glass case and it was kept for years in the children's bedroom. Later the stuffed ape was burned on a bonfire in either Dudley or Horseley Heath."

Chris Whitcombe also has a story about the ape. Now living in Wiltshire he happened to be in Wolverhampton when he picked up a copy of the *Express and Star* and was amazed to read the article on my family's connections with the Tipton Slasher – for Christopher, too, has been brought up with tales of a relationship with Bill Perry. Chris's gran was a Lillian Perry. She lived on the Coventry Road in Birmingham with her husband John Whitcombe, before moving to Wiltshire to be near to her son and grandson. Born in 1893 she always declared that she was related directly to the Tipton Slasher, because her grandfather, James, was a younger brother to the famed fighter.

Her own father was a William Perry. He was born in 1866 and died before he was 30. Years ago, at a talk I gave in Bromsgrove, I met a Doreen J. Rowland, a cousin of Chris's and I have just come across her letter to me. She related that William was married to a Miss Long and that when cycling to work he caught rheumatic fever and died. After his death, William's wife, Eliza Kate, would not allow the name of Bill Perry to be mentioned in the house, because she declared that he was "a disgusting fighting man who drank heavily".

Still the odd story did get passed on to her daughter, Lillian. In particular Chris recalls that "Gran said she used to go to a relation who had a pub over West Bromwich way where there was a stuffed monkey over the top of the bar and she remembers asking about it and being told that it was Bill's monkey." The William Perry who was Chris's great grandfather, was born in 1866 and it seems that his father, James – the brother of the Tipton Slasher – died whilst his children were young. By 1881, his widow, Ellen, was the head of the family and was living with her children – Emily, William, Thomas and Frederick – in a back-to-back house in Vaughton Street in Highgate, Birmingham.

This is only a spitting distance from where my Grandad, Arthur Perry, was raised in the early twentieth century. Doing some research into the family history over the last couple of weeks it looks like my Grandad's father, Thomas, was born in Farley Street, West Bromwich in 1879. In turn, his father, another William who was the nephew of the Tipton Slasher, was born in 1851 in Tipton itself. It would seem from all these Williams that because of the success of Bill Perry his Christian name was given to several of his nephews.

Mrs M. Sharman notes that the ape was on display in the 'Prince Regent' in Horseley Heath, Tipton. This was kept by George Budgen who is shown in the photo with Jack Fisher who lived in Park Lane East and whose "wife used to play the piano at the Prince Regent on weekends. My Mom used to clean for Mr Budgen and I also used to work for him as a waitress when I was fifteen". That was fifty odd years ago and Mrs Sharman thinks that Mr Budgen passed the ape on to someone else.

Gary Gibbons believes that "the true story about the ape goes that the ape was killed by the Slasher's father who knocked it down a flight of stairs after being bitten on the finger. So distressed was the Slasher that he had it stuffed. It was passed on to his great-granddaughter Mrs Elizabeth Harding of the Three Horseshoes in Ocker Hill who gave it to the licensee of the Horseley Heath pub when she retired in 1940 and then it was ceremoniously burnt at the rear of the pub in the early 1960s."

However, Jenni Crawford, nee Clazey, queries whether the ape was burned on a bonfire. Back in 1970, her first post after leaving school was as a display artist for Dudley Museums and Art Galleries, "a job I adored, because of its variety and local history connections. I turned my hand to most things, from creating a Jackson Pollock look-a-like for one exhibition, to cleaning Civic plate for another." Jenni recalls the Museum's local history gallery and was well acquainted with many artefacts "as it was my and my boss's job to collate and clean them".

Now one day Jenni was called "to come and look at a stuffed animal that had been donated to the museum with an enamel belt that I was informed was a Lonsdale Belt belonging to The Tipton Slasher, a bare knuckle fighter. The animal was indeed a monkey of about 2 feet high posing in exactly the same pose that your picture of him in the pub revealed. Having gone across the road to the library I found out more about the Slasher and the story behind the monkey." Aged just sixteen or seventeen, Jenni was photographed with the monkey which had been donated to the museum by a Sedgley woman who had emigrated to Australia.

Mick McNally has a tale to tell of a descendant of the Tipton Slasher. He used to go to Saint Joseph's Roman Catholic School in Wolverhampton where the headmaster was Mr Morgan. He "was so proud of his boxing team, about the best in Wolverhampton, and one day he was addressing the school in the assembly hall about how the team had done well as usual, but a team that always had the edge on us was a Tipton School. At that Mr Morgan stated about the legend of the

Tipton Slasher. A pupil put his hand up with 'Please Sir'. Mr Morgan not being too pleased with being interrupted said, 'What is it boy?' Mr Morgan was a good headmaster not much more than 5' 4" but you cross him. 'This better be worth it boy, what is it?' 'Please sir', said the pupil named Perry, 'That's my great grandad'. The hall rocked with laughter. 'Right', said Mr Morgan, 'Put his name down for the boxing team.'"

Dr Carl Chinn views a plaque in memory of the author, David Christie Murray, at Sandwell Central Library, West Bromwich.

One of the last people to speak with the Tipton Slasher before he died was the author David Christie Murray. Born in 1847 in the High Street, West Bromwich, Murray began as a journalist on the old Wednesbury Advertiser. He became a noted war correspondent and also wrote a number of novels. One of them A Capful O' Nails (1896) is a powerful and moving account of the hard lives of the Black Country nailmakers. In his autobiography, Making of a Novelist (1894), Murray explained that he was a lover of "the noble art of self defence" and stated that "the very first man who helped me with a pair of boxing gloves was the mighty 'Slasher' – the Tipton Slasher".

In his youth Murray used to visit Bill Perry in his pub, against the vehement wishes of his father: "I have been put on bread and water and held in solitary confinement for the same misdemeanour, but the man had a glamour for me and drew me with the attraction of a magnet." Murray described the Slasher as "a Hercules of a man, with enormous shoulders, and his rough, honest mid-England features had a sort of surly welcome in their look. But for an odd deformity he would have had the stature of a giant; but he was hideously knock-kneed, and his shamble when he walked was awkward to the limits of grotesque. You have only to invert the letter V to have an idea of the Slasher's legs from foot to knee. His feet were strangers to each other, but his knees were inseparable friends, and hugged each other in a perpetual intimacy.

"In fighting he used to await his man, propped up in this inverted V fashion, and somehow he gained so solid a footing in that strange and clumsy attitude that he never, in all his experience of the Ring, received a knock-down blow until he encountered Tom Sayers in that last melancholy fight which cost him the championship, and the snug little property in the Champion of England public house, and his friends, and his reputation, and all he had in the world."

During his adulthood Murray did not see Bill Perry until the day of the death of the big man. On that occasion the old fighter's "vast chest and shoulders were shrunken and bowed, so that one wondered where the very framework of the giant had fallen to." No longer did adoring crowds gather around him and he seemed alone, his wife Anne-Marie having died but a few months before. Murray chatted with Bill Perry and the Tipton man's thoughts were on his last fight. "They mought ha' let me aloon. I'd held the belt for seventeen 'ear. They mought ha' let me aloon. Tum's a good un. I've sin 'em all, an' I've niver sin a better. But he owed to ha' let me be. Theer was no credit to be got in hommerin' a man at my time o' life.

"All the same, mind ye, I thowt I should ha' trounced him. So I should if I could ha' got at him; but he fled hither an' he fled thither, and he was about me like a cooper a-walkin' round a cask. An' I was fule enough to lose temper, an' the crowd begun to laugh an' gibe at me an' I took to raercin' round after him, an' my wind went, an' where was I then? He knocked me down – fair an' square he did it. Th'on'y time it iver chanced to me. I put everythin' I had o' that fight, an' here I bin."

These were the last known words of Bill Perry, the Tipton Slasher.

This photo of the statue of the Tipton Slasher in Coronation Gardens (right) was given to me by Freda Perry. Freda's husband came from Tipton "and he always said that his Father was a cousin of the Tipton Slasher". Both Freda and her husband were at the unveiling ceremony of the statue in 1993. The statue itself was the result of a successful campaign to honour the Tipton Slasher that was kicked off by a group of Tiptonians that included Martin Collinson, Steve Woodward, Peter Golding and Jim Holland. They were supported by the Tipton Civic Society, the Tipton and Coseley Building Society, the Black Country Society, the Tipton Boxing Club, Sandwell Council and the Black Country Living Museum.

A Tipton Slasher appeal was soon started, of which Jim Holland was the chairman. Other key figures on the appeal committee included Councillor Brett Bates and Chris Martin, and it was backed wholeheartedly in its efforts by John Brimble JP – well known for his devotion to the history of Tipton – Keith Hodgkins and Ian Walden OBE. At first the group wanted to bring Bill Perry's remains from Saint John's Churchyard, Kate's Hill in Dudley to Tipton. This idea was abandoned and efforts then focused on erecting a life-size statue to

The Tipton Slasher Statue shortly after its opening.

be placed in Coronation Gardens, alongside the cut upon which the Tipton Slasher worked and overlooking his headquarters of the 'Fountain Inn'.

The £25,000 needed for the bronze statue was raised in just seven months and was proof of the determination of the appeal committee and the affinity of Tiptonians with their local hero. Produced by Tipton artist Bill Haynes, the striking statue of the Tipton Slasher in a fighting pose was cast at Lunt's Foundry in Handsworth, Birmingham and stands on a plinth of red and blue brick. It was unveiled on Spring Bank Holiday Monday, 3 May, 1993 and over 1,000 people turned up to see the unveiling by the Mayor of Sandwell, Councillor John Sullivan.

I would like to pay tribute to the research and lore of Tom Langley who wrote the definitive life story of the Tipton Slasher, and which has been invaluable in writing these article.

Chapter 2

AN INDUSTRIAL HERITAGE
WHICH HAS MADE ITS MARK

It was not a journey that was relished by Robert Southey, the man of letters who was later to find fame as Poet Laureate. There he was in 1803 on the long and tiresome trip from London to the Lake District, where he was to say with his brother-in-law, Samuel Taylor Coleridge, another celebrated poet. Stifled with fifteen other passengers in a long horse-pulled coach, he deplored the fact that he was enveloped in an oppressive atmosphere like that of a prison. Mardy and mithered, he arrived in Birmingham where he was made giddy and dizzy by the "hammering of presses, the clatter of engines, the whirling of wheels".

His head aching from "a multiplicity of noises" and his eyes sore with "the light of infernal fires", he was keen to move on quickly and after just a day and night in Brum, he took a place on a fast mail coach to Manchester. It was a fair morning and Southey sat on the roof, joyous at freeing himself from the heavy cloud of smoke that hung over Birmingham and hopeful that he was travelling into a better atmosphere.

Heading west towards Wolverhampton, his high expectations were shattered on the anvil of industry. Everywhere, the "tower of some manufactory was to be seen in the distance, vomiting up flames and smoke, and blasting every thing around with metallic vapours". The whole district was "as thickly peopled as that of London" and the houses were all blackened with the smoke of coal fires that burned both day and night. The poetic sensibilities of Southey were repelled by the marks of hard collar, and he declaimed the face of the country as "more hideous than can be described, uncultivated, black and smoking".

No-one knows who first coined the name the Black Country, but this unflattering description by an unsympathetic outsider raised in fashionable Bath and educated at Oxford, is one of the first to associate blackness with the Black Country – and it is interesting that he uses the adjective black to describe not only the face of the countryside but also its buildings.

A generation later, the Scottish historian and writer Thomas Carlyle reinforced the dark look of the Black Country and its people. In 1824, Carlyle passed several weeks in Birmingham with his friend, John Badams, a manufacturer of vitriol. One

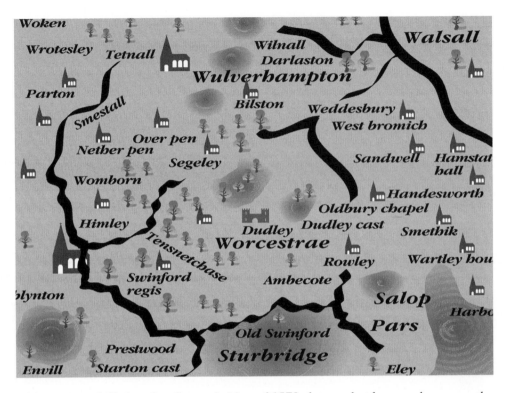

This section of Christopher Saxton's Map of 1579 shows what became known as the Black Country and is included in a most significant book by Eric Richardson called The Black Country as seen through Antique Maps, A Survey from 1579 (2000). A pioneering work it is published by the Black Country Society and gives a geographical reality to the term The Black Country.

August day, he and three other companions left Brummagem for the neighbourhood of iron and coal works – "a half frightful scene!" It would seem that he was on the southern side of the Black Country for he declared that "a space perhaps of 30 square miles to the north of us, was covered over with furnaces, rolling-mills, steam-engines and sooty men". A dense cloud of pestilential smoke hung over the district, "blackening even the grain that grows upon it; and at night the whole region burns like a volcano spitting fire from a thousand tubes of brick". In the coal mines locally, the colliers were "black as ravens", whilst the men who toiled in the blast furnaces were "besmeared with soot".

Twelve years later in *Birmingham and its Vicinity*, William Hawkes Smith affirmed the black nature of the area, proclaiming that its inhabitants were "consistently employed in mining and in blackening manufactures" and that they

The smoke rising from the Bradley Ironworks in 1836 from a painting by Robert Noyes, which is in the William Salt Library in Stafford.

were united by "a peculiarity of manner, habit and language". Still, though Hawkes Smith emphasised the blackness of industrial, he did not use the term the Black Country. By contrast, Carlyle did – although many years after his visit. In his *Reminiscences* penned in 1881, the Scot recalled how powerfully he had been affected by what he had seen to the west of Birmingham, and also brought to mind an earlier trip in July 1824. On that occasion, he and Badams galloped from Birmingham over to Hagley and the top of Clent Hill. Half way along, the friends came into a "wholly Metallic Country", of which Hales Owen was the heart. From the top of the hill were visible many smoke pillars "in a definite, straight or spiral shape – the Dudley Black Country under favourable omens".

Was then Carlyle the first to actually use the name the Black Country as opposed to describing the landscape and the workers as black? No, he was not. So who was then? Well, Charles J. L. Elwell is an important and assiduous researcher into the history of the Black Country and a regular contributor to the *Blackcountryman*, the journal of the Black Country Society. In one of his essays he reveals that the publication *Punch* used the term the Black Country in December 1866 and did so in a derogatory fashion. (See *Black Country Essays and Reviews*, 1998). Two years later a positive depiction of the Black Country and its people was given by Elihu Burritt in *Walks in the Black Country and its Green Hinterland*. The American Consul to Birmingham, Burritt was a dedicated campaigner for peace and against slavery. Indeed he was appointed to his position by Abraham Lincoln and took it up two months after the assassination of the president.

Living in Harborne, Burritt was enjoined to report on the trade of the United States of America with his consular district and to add facts about its productive capacities, industrial character and natural resources. Burritt soon realised that a few pages appended to each report would not be enough to draw out the characteristics of the West Midlands and so he wrote *Walks in the Black Country*. It is a fascinating

The Black Country in the 1960s. This was another photo about which there was little information, but Express and Star readers again quickly identified the place. Keith Cherrington of Tividale was really stirred by this photo and he told me that it was taken at what used to be Lockside in Tipton. This was the bottom lock at the top of Griffith Street looking towards Union Street and Albion Street with Lee Howle's stack in the distance. The girl shown is Theresa Cave, who is with her brother Ian who was about three then. They also lived in Griffith Street. Theresa herself would have been about twelve at the time the picture was taken. Keith used to live round the corner from Griffith Street in what was Queens Road and adds that "the large stone where the children are standing is still in position to-day".

I would also like to thank Mrs V. Coleman of Beehive Walk, Tipton for her information about this photo of the canal locks in Tipton, alongside which were Theresa and Ian Caves. Mrs Coleman tells me that the locks ran from the old Beehive pub in Elliot Road to the Conservative Club in Union Street.

and insightful work that includes vital information not only on manufacturing, trade and commerce but also on public buildings, prominent figures, historical events and natural history. And it also includes one of the most compelling and vivid descriptions of "this remarkable district", the Black Country.

One night, Burritt and a companion secured entry to Dudley Castle. After warily climbing the deep-worn and winding steps that closely hugged the circular wall, they reached the parapet where "a grand panorama burst upon us". Proclaiming that the best poet of the nation should put his genius under the influence of that spectacle, Burritt went on to draw a scene "which cannot be paralleled on the globe". A military writer might have said that "it was the sublimest battle-scene ever enacted on earth; that ten thousand Titans were essaying to breach heaven with a thousand mortars, each charged with a small, red-hot hill".

Fixing his eyes to the north from his vantage point, Burritt looked down across the settlements of the Tame Valley. Half circled as this space was by the Sedgley-Rowley ridge on which he stood, the low ground beneath him was also closed in by hills at its northern edge – and upon which stood towns like Darlaston and Wednesbury. The whole prospect made:

an embattled amphitheatre of twenty miles span ridged to the purple clouds. Planted at artillery intervals on this encircling ridge, and at musket-shot spaces in the dark valley between, a thousand batteries, mounted with huge ordnance, white at the mouth with the fury of the bombardment, were pouring their cross-fires of shot and shell into the cloud works of the lower heavens.

Wolverhampton, on the extreme left, stood by her black mortars which shot their red volleys into the night. Coseley and Bilston and Wednesbury replied bomb for bomb and set the clouds on fire above with their lighted matches. Oldbury, Albion, and Smethwick, on the right plied their heavy breachers at the iron-works on the other side; while West Bromwich and distant Walsall showed that their men were standing as bravely to their guns, and that their guns were charged to the muzzle with the grape and canister of the mine. The canals, twisting and crossing through the field of battle, showed by patches in the light like bleeding veins.

At the right centre of the line, the Brades Works of Oldbury discharged a thousand spades, hoes, trowels and pruning hooks each hour; whilst further towards Birmingham "there was a well-manned battery that poured forth a shower of bolts and nuts; and Chance's great fortress was all ablaze, with its hot fountains sending out acres of glass to be parcelled into pans of every size". Indeed, the whole arena of action was working for the world, producing the thousand small arms of peace – from cotton hoes for Brazil to Harpoons for the Behring Straits, "and, for all the countries between, every tool used in honest labour".

Burritt regarded Birmingham as the metropolis of the Black Country, but for all the deep interdependency between the two places then and now you'd be hard put to find either a Black Country chap or Brummagem bloke who would believe that Birmingham is in the Black Country. Amongst the principal towns of the Black Country, Burritt numbered Dudley, Wolverhampton, Willenhall, Halesowen, Oldbury, West Bromwich, Wednesbury, Wednesfield, Bilston, Tipton, Sedgley, Walsall, Smethwick and Stourbridge.

The last two are contentious. Many of us regard Smethwick as neither one nor t'other, but as somewhere special in its own right as the fulcrum between the Black Country and Birmingham. Similarly, Stourbridge is often perceived as just outside the Black Country – despite the significance of its glass works and fire clay, and even though The Lye, which adjoins it, is seen as part of the Black Country. Furthermore, some people might argue that both Wolverhampton and Walsall are not really Black Country towns.

So if commentators wrote of the Black Country as a distinct place from the mid-nineteenth century and named it so because of its murky atmosphere and blackened appearance, where exactly was this Black Country? Writing in 1883, the celebrated engineer James Nasmyth recalled the occasion 53 years before when he had left Shifnal and traipsed southwards. Arriving at Dudley, he asserted confidently that "I was in the middle of the Black Country". Few people would disagree as to the centrality of Dudley to the concept of the Black Country as much as to its physicality.

Nasmyth's portrayal also indicated another reason why the region was called black, because "the earth seems to have been turned inside out. Its entrails are strewn about; nearly the entire surface of the ground is covered with cinder-heaps and mounds of scoriae. The coal, which has been drawn from below ground, is blazing on the surface."

There can be no doubt that coal was crucial to the emergence of the Black Country. Its digging scarred and blackened the ground and its burning blackened both the air and the faces of working folk. Allowing for the fact that Dudley and Oldbury were Worcestershire islands and Halesowen a Shropshire isle all surrounded by Staffordshire, then perhaps the South Staffordshire coalfield may be taken as the determinant of the extent of the Black Country. This coalfield begins at the Bentley Fault in the north, which separates it from the Cannock Chase coalfield. As a result Walsall, Willenhall and Darlaston are brought firmly within the Black Country – as are Bilston, Bradeley, Moxley, Wednesfield and Wednesbury. But does that mean that Bloxwich is just across the border or just within it? And what about Pelsall and Shelfield?

Wolverhampton emerges as on the limits of the Black Country, straddling as it does the Western Boundary Fault of the coalfield, whilst West Bromwich, including Hamstead and its mine as well as Hill Top and other neighbourhoods, takes up a similar position on the Eastern Boundary Fault. Centrally placed are Tipton, Coseley, Oldbury, Tividale, Langley and Dudley, of course; whilst to the south are gathered Rowley, Pensnett, the Gornals, Cradley Heath, Cradley, The Lye, Netherton, Old Hill and Brierley Hill – all of which are clearly within the Black Country. Sedgley meanwhile lies towards the western edge of the district – as does Kingswinford – with Wordsley, Amblecote, Stourbridge and Halesowen hard on the southern limits, perhaps in the Black Country to some and just outside to others.

But the Black Country was and is more than a place defined by minerals and work. Hawkes Smith understood that almost 170 years ago when he identified something singular about the people of the Black Country, fastened together as they were by "a peculiarity of manner, habit and language". For a place is as nothing and can be nothing without its people. Carved out by their landscape as much as they carved it out in the digging of coal, limestone, fire clay and iron ore, forged by their manufactures as much as they forged the metals crucial to their industries, the folk of the Black Country are bonded together by their sense of place, their understanding of their past, their awareness of their culture and their pride in their language. Because of these strong characteristics, the Black Country is a place that becomes more than a place, infused as it is with a spirit that reaches out from those who have gone before to those yet unborn. For both, those living are the custodians of the Black Country.

A powerful and evocative view of the Black Country from near to Rowley Regis in the 1950s and featured in my Black Country Memories feature in the Express and Star. All that was known about it was that it was taken near to Rowley Regis in the 1950s. Well, thanks to Express and Star readers, the exact spot was identified.

Mrs Johnson rang in the day after the article appeared to say that the view on the previous page was taken from the Dudley Road at Springfield, with Cromwell Street on the right. The double-fronted building in the right-hand bottom corner is Cooksey's corner shop and off-licence, where her mother used to take her jugs to be filled with beer. Then where the gable end is of a dark building on the far left there was a butcher's; whilst the chimney stacks in the foreground were Doulton's sanitary ware factory.

Reg Oerton adds that Cromwell Street used to lead into Springfield Lane, commonly known as Bayley's Hill, whilst John Adams points out that the photo would have been taken from the area of the footpath on the Dudley Road, about 200 yards east of Wendover Road. This footpath goes to the top of Turner's Hill.

Springfield Lane itself runs from the left across the picture, leading to Bullpits Farm which would be just off the photo and centre right. The far centre stacks are Hingley's Iron Works in Netherton and Netherton Church would be near the top right-hand corner.

Dan Shakespeare recalls that to get down into Cromwell Street from the Dudley Road "you had to descend quite a lot of steps, and when you got to the bottom you felt you were in the bowels of the earth." Dan's Aunt Alice and Uncle Joe Darby lived in the first house on the right and if you carried on down Cromwell Street you came into Blackberry Lane, "turn left and it took you back up the main road by Bailey's Post Office and the Hailstone pub. Turn right and you could cross the bridge over the canal and you could walk up to Netherton." When they were lads, Dan and his pals used to swim in the cut and "we also crossed over the bridge, hanging on by our finger tips. We never thought of falling in."

Mike Ruston was also surprised to see a photo of the street in which he was born in 1946 – and he is also a Darby through his mom, Alice, a daughter of Alice and Joe, who was married to Sam Ruston. The Rustons lived in the house on the right, which has the gable end facing us. Across the way and just below Cooksey's outdoor lived Jenny Harris, another daughter of Joe and Alice, with her husband Jack.

Michael's mom told him that they were related to the famous Josie 'the Jumper' Darby and remembered that "on one Winter's night, Grandad Darby fetched his beer from Cooksey's and fell, losing all his beer in the snow. Times were so hard he couldn't afford any more until the following Saturday."

All these houses have now gone and have been replaced by a new estate, except for a few off Springfield Lane. These surviving houses mean a lot to Richard Hadley. He was born in Springfield in 1942 and has lived there most of his life. In fact he still lives in a house that was built by his father for his maternal grandparents. In them days, Springfield was a village in its own right and "anybody from Rowley was foreigners". As for Mr Cooksey of the shop, "he was a real character. When you went in the shop and it'd be empty you hit the bell, and then you'd hear him coming humming along. And he had a big old moustache. If anyone wanted Beecham's Powder you'd get them from there, and a bit of grocery but it was more on the sweets."

Richard has sat for days examining the photo with his magnifying glass and has revealed some vital information. In the centre of the scene is a telegraph pole upon a mound, to the left of which are three men. This was the quarry tip, down the incline of which on the other side lay the canal. Further along, just beyond the man in the white shirt, is Bullfields Bridge, whilst the railway runs right across the middle of the photo. Before Richard's day, there were watercress fields in the low ground on the left, and even when he was growing up there were a number of springs locally – harking back to why the area was called Springfield. And he confirms that there was a butcher's owned by the Neil family in the terrace on the left and that a grandson of the family now runs a butcher's shop in Blackheath High Street. The chimneys in the background are those of Hingley's and Danks's, whilst those in the foreground belonged to Doulton's – where the Doulton Trading Estate is today. This is where Richard's parents both worked. His Mom, born Mary Hingley, used to put the white glaze on sinks and toilets, whilst his father, Dick, realigned all the kilns after they fired and emptied – and the sulphur and the stink from them kilns was fierce.

Connie Palmer, Connie Parsons as was then, was as chuffed as Richard and Mrs Johnson to see this view – so much so that she rang me up on BBC WM to chat about it. She was born in the end house of Cromwell Street, on the right-hand side of the photo, and when she was young the postal address was Cromwell Street, Springfield near Dudley. The house had just two bedrooms upstairs and "nine of us kids were born there. It brought back a lot of memories. Everybody was poor and there were lots of pits there. It's amazing what you can see there in the photo which you can't even see there now. Right across the canal you can see Saint Peter's Church, Windmill End."

Connie points out that everyone was in the same boat in the hard days of the 1930s when the Means Test Man preyed upon working-class families. Her dad was a miner and then did labouring jobs, doing what he could to earn money. As the oldest child, Connie would often go "across the banks picking coal. There were three pits I know of in Springfield. There'd be lots of us all picking coal, putting it into pushchairs and prams. Mom was a poor, hard-working soul. We were all loved and mother never went out to work. She stayed at home to look after us."

Pam Richards, nee Bingham, of Rowley Regis was excited to see the back of her garden in Springfield Lane, where the three men are sitting by the gable end wall. She was born there in 1944. E. Bowater of Rowley Regis also lived locally and notes that the houses in the centre of the picture were in Springfield

Lane, which led from 'The Knowle' in Springfield. The embankment running from left to right across the centre was the railway line which went form Old Hill to Dudley, whilst the NCB Canal is shown just below the embankment on the right-hand side.

Terry Haywood, now of Halesowen, has gone over the photo with a fine comb and helpfully numbered places on a copy of the photo for me. At the top of Cromwell Street on the right lived the Darbys, below which were Cooksey's outdoor, the Randalls and the Harris family. Turning left at the bottom of Cromwell Street into Springfield Lane – in the houses running across the middle of the photo – lived the Farmers, Bishops, Bowaters, Binghams – who were Terry's aunt and uncle – and the Davis family. Then came Mrs Harper – who was Terry's grandmother and who ran a sweet and grocery shop from her house, number 14A.

Next up were the Paynes and Rudges, followed by the Haywoods at number 17. Terry was born there in 1942 and lived there until 1960 when the area was knocked down. Their neighbour was Neil and King the butchers, known as Jackie Kings. As well as Hingley's and Danks's in the distance, Terry has identified Swindells Shovel Works. He himself worked at Noah Hingley's chain and anchor

The completed Chapel Fields flats, an impressive sight on the Dudley skyline when approached from Quarry Bank. In the late 1960s the tower blocks were built to replace many sub-standard houses in Hill Street, Chapel Street, Derry Street, South Street, Brickkiln Street and Potter Street. In the distance is the Round Oaks steelworks, top centre, and Delph Road at the bottom.

works as an apprentice between 1957 and 1966 and he can still remember most of the works – the chainmaking, forging and the rest.

Mick Day of West Bromwich recalls many of the stories that were passed on to him by his late father, who would be 98 now and was Greets Green born and bred. In particular, he remembers that "The Black Country got its name from the Staffordshire coal seam that runs right through the spine of the Black Country, thirty feet down under the Town Hall in West Brom High Street being the thickest part of the seam. As you know Carl, people in Brum and the Black Country had large families, to say the least, and my old man was the youngest of nine. Many of his stories, I suppose, were passed on through the years. There was no tele or radio then, just conversation. He wore clogs till he left school, saved his money and bought his first pair of shoes at the age of thirteen."

John Cunliffe of Coseley has a strong memory "of the corn fields on the Rocket Pool Estate, Bradley and when they started to develop the land for houses and when they started to dig the ground there was lots of coal. So I was sent by my parents to collect coal for our fire at home. The name Black Country came about because of all the factories in and around Bradley, Bilston, Darlaston, Wednesbury and Dudley because of all the smoke from their chimneys. I wonder if any of your readers remembers some of the factories like Sankey's, Tipper's the glass factor, Perry's foundry, The Cannon, and all those. They were big companies that employed hundreds of people. I myself worked at Tipper's in Bradley from the age of fifteen for twenty years."

Mrs Gladys Dumelow of Willenhall has written to me about the definition of what and where is the Black Country. Before the Second World War, when she was in her senior years at Hillary Street School, Pleck, Walsall, her history teacher was a Mr Lambert: "Now he made us learn how the Black Country got its name. I can't remember the date but it was when the Midlands was only farms and forests, no fire engines and not too many people. There had been a long, hot summer and somewhere near the far side of Dudley a fire started and the wind blew it hither and thither and no-one could stop it spreading, burning everything in its path.

"He had a large map that he hung on the blackboard and he was a very strict teacher. We had to try and copy this map and if you put the towns affected in the wrong place you had the tawse – boy or girl, it made no difference. I remember that a small part of Aldridge was included but definitely no part of Wolverhampton. The fire was only put out by a big rainfall." The blackened earth from the fire gave the name the Black Country.

Allan Savage of Willenhall was prompted to write this poem by my article discussing where is the Black Country.

The Black Country

There's a question that's bin puzzling me
Where is the capital of the Black Country?
I know it aye our best mate Brum,
Although it is if yoe listen tew some.
But tham from down south so they doe know nuthin
About bercun and grey paes, or grorty pudding.
Of shift thee big shommochs from up the ess ole
Or that a raker's a big lump of coal.
Sew whilst on their opinion I'll cast a frown
Some say the capital's Dudley town.
Now Dudley might be bostin un pretty
Surely a capital should be a city.
There is a plerce with city status
However there's a slight hiatus,
There used to be a school of thought
That Amptun in the Black Country wort.
It's no wonder the capital's hard tew find
When the Black Country itself cor be defined.
So after some research un cank
I reckon the Black Country capital is in the bank.

Chapter 3

THE BLACK STUFF WHICH LAID THE FOUNDATIONS FOR REVOLUTION

Coal. Its burning in furnaces and factories blazed Britain into industrial supremacy, on locomotives and steam ships it transformed travel, and in gas works it created a new power whose huge holders dominated the industrial landscape. If the Industrial Revolution made Britain the unrivalled economic force in the world by 1851, then it was coal that made the Industrial Revolution. And in that remarkable change the men and women who laboured above and below ground in the South Staffordshire coalfield were crucial figures.

The dominating feature of this coalfield was the Ten Yard Seam. Properly known as Thick Coal, in reality this was made up of between ten and fourteen seams. Beneath most of the Black Country these were so closely overlaid that they gave the appearance of one coal bed. North of the Russell Hall Fault, which runs

The Arch of Coal at Queen Victoria's visit to Wolverhampton in 1866, Illustrated London News.

south east from Gornal to Rowley, the Thick Coal was mostly 400 feet or less beneath the surface. This embraced the mines of Dudley, Coseley, Bilston, Darlaston and Wednesbury, and gave them a distinction – for nowhere else in Britain was such a crop of coal so shallow. Indeed, in and around Wednesbury the ten yard seam actually rose to the surface, leading to open-cast mining. Just 21 miles long at its furthest extent and generally between six and seven miles in breadth, the South Staffordshire coalfield was small but yet in the middle years of the nineteenth century it was second only to the vast Northern Coalfield in national importance. So widespread were the mines across this region that they overwhelmed the whole district and staggered visitors.

In 1843, Thomas Tancred visited the Black Country for the Midland Mining Commission. He felt that he was passing through an "interminable village" for he was never out of sight of cottages and two-storey houses. These houses, "for the most part, are not arranged in continuous streets, but are interspersed with blazing furnaces, heaps of burning coal in process of coking, piles of iron stone calcining, forges, pit-banks, and engine-chimneys; the country being besides intersected with canals, crossing each other at various levels, and the small remaining patches of the surface-soil occupied with irregular fields of grass or corn, intermingled with heaps of the refuse of mines, or of slag from the blast-furnaces."

Working at the Ten Yard Seam, about 1890. The picture was used in the Final Part of the Miners' Eight Hour Day Committee, published in 1907.

Man and beast in perfect harmony – miners and pit ponies at one of the Dibdale Collieries in Dudley, possibly Russell's Hall, between 1870 and 1890.

Tancred went on to describe how sometimes a road passed between mounds of pit waste as if it were a deep railway cutting. Elsewhere the road would be like a causeway, raised above the fields on either side, which had subsided because of excavations for coal. In one place the road actually sloped markedly on the one edge. Tancred asked his driver why it was not repaired and was told that the coal beneath was still worked and so "they would probably wait to see if the road would not right itself by sinking on the opposite side, and so become level again".

The effect of so many mines was to make the Black Country like a "vast rabbit-warren" where it was an everyday occurrence for houses "to fall down or a row of buildings inhabited by numerous families to assume a very irregular outline, from what they call a swag, caused by the sinking of the ground into old workings". Of course, 'The Glynne Arms', better known as 'The Crooked House' or 'The Siden House' is misshapen because of the same process noticed by Tancred over 160 years ago.

There was another intriguing result of mining locally. Early potatoes for the London market were grown near Dudley because of the warmth given off by the steam and smoke emanating from an old colliery which was disused but which was on fire. Because the coal could be reached more easily, the South Staffordshire coalfield developed in a unique way. Small coal masters were plentiful and their workers used mining techniques that were peculiar to the Black Country. Crucial to the whole process were men known as holers. Using light picks, they sat on their haunches beneath the Ten Yard Seam and hewed a hole into the bottom measures of the coal. They stopped when they reached the natural

Princes End Colliery, Tipton, towards the end of the nineteenth century. This photo of the colliery at Princess End, Tipton led Doug Cox to drop me a note. Now best known for the family firm of Purity Soft Drinks Limited of Wednesbury, he tells me that his father, Benjamin, and uncle, Joseph, once owned this pit. Benjamin was raised in Tividale, and like many working-class youngsters he left school to go to work before he was fourteen because he passed the Labour Exam. He went down the pit and later took on the Princess End Colliery, where there is now an ASDA supermarket, and others on Cannock Chase.

The Princess End pit was closed in late 1919 because of flooding when the South Staffordshire Mines Drainage Commissioners ordered "the cessation of the pumping operations of the Commissioners in the Tipton District". In a letter dated 27th February 1920, the two brothers wrote to the Commissioners explaining that because of the action "serious loss ensued to us by this enforced abandonment of our underground roadways which had been driven at considerable expense, and by which the mining of the Thick Coal Seam was rendered possible for an extensive period.

"The actual flooding of the mines also prevented the removal of the quantity of rails, tools and stores, thereby adding to the heavy loss sustained. We are practical men, who have not only been deprived of a large portion of our capital, but also of the possibility of reopening the fruit of our skill and industry unstintingly applied over a lengthy time." This evidence reminds us that many of the mines in the Black Country were leased and run not by great landlords but by smaller enterprises created by people who grafted to get what they had – and had not inherited it.

parting between the lower level and that above it. To support the massive weight of coal above them they built up cogs of stones.

Once enough coal had been undermined, the holers then cut a gap between that section which was to fall and that which was intended to stand. In effect a pillar was formed to support the roof of the mine. Such pillars were made at both sides of the mass that was to fall and also at the end where it still joined the solid coal. At the same time, small supports called spurns connected the undermined coal with the pillars. The cutting finished, the most skilful holer then hacked at and broke away the cogs and spurns with a long pick so that tons of coal fell down.

It is little wonder that mining was called the "hardest work under heaven", for the holers, or pikemen as they were also known, collared in a claustrophobic, oppressive and dangerous space. When it was finished a hole would be, perhaps, six foot long, three foot wide and just two foot three inches high. Young and fit, the holers might have to graft for eight or nine hours to finish their stint, contorting their bodies as they sat to pick away at the coal. Only the flickering light of candles tentatively challenged the utter darkness, whilst the only sound was the grunting of the holers as they shifted position or struck at the coal.

After the coal had fallen it was shifted by bondsmen. Paid a flat rate for a twelve hour day and not by the stint (area holed) or the piece as were the pikemen, these chaps included the turners out, who broke the massive pieces of coal, and the loaders, who put the broken coal onto skips. Then pitchers, lads as young as twelve, enclosed the coal with iron hoops after which the skip was pulled along iron tramways by a horse led by its driver until it reached the bottom of the shaft. Here labourers called hangers on attached the load of coal by means of a hook to a flat rope called a band – hence the term bandsmen or bondsmen – or else to a chain, following which it was hoisted above ground.

The band of miners was made up by dirt carriers, whose job was to shovel up into baskets or iron trays with a handle the small coal dust that was not good enough to take to the surface. Such slack was carried from where the holers were straining their whole beings to an empty space further back. In this gob, a clancer or cleanser separated the stony partings of the coal.

With the mass of coal removed, the pikeman could then stand upright and start to hack into the next level of the ten yard seam. When the upper levels were out of reach scaffolding was put up. Once again, the pikeman was condemned to labour in harsh and exhausting conditions. In his visit to the Black Country, Tancred went down the pit at Heath Colliery, West Bromwich. He pitied the pikemen at their endless task, remarking that working from the scaffold was "much more severe labour than holing". Their upper body and arms were exerted so strenuously to cut a channel in the heat of the mine that one pikeman declared that sweat streamed from them like rain. Deep beneath the earth and away from

An indication of the smaller-sized pits in operation – Rowley Regis colliery at the turn of the twentieth century.

the strength of the sun, still it was as hot as a summer's day, so much so that many of the pikemen worked naked, covered only by coal dust.

Tancred sought for his readers to feel the predicament of the pikeman by asking them to suppose that the ceiling of a room was a stratum of coal nearly four foot thick. The pikeman dug into the ceiling and slowly carved out a channel about a foot wide alongside the side of the wall. Now if he cut that channel along the length of the ceiling it would collapse for lack of support and kill the pikeman. Accordingly, every six foot or so the miner left part of the coal uncut. This was a spurn. Eventually when the channel had been cut as deep as the pikeman could possibly achieve, usually about four feet, the lower edge of the cutting was made bigger. All the while, the miner ensured that one side of the channel was straight, whilst that side on which the coal was to fall was sloping. This done, the pikemen would make a channel upon the other side of the 'ceiling', and when he had finished the spurns in both channels could be knocked down so that the coal between them would fall.

Specialist pikemen carried out this task, using 'prickers', long-handled pointers that pushed and pricked at the spurns. This process was called throwing the coal and it was a most dangerous operation, as one pikeman expressively brought to the fore. In his account he mentions the butties. These were the middle men who were contracted by the mine owners for a piece of work, out of which sum they paid their men and made their profit. Many of the butties pressurised their lads into working fast and taking risks so that they could make more money. The pikeman explained:

I was working last night at throwing coal. It's safer at night, because when the horses, and rings, and skips are making a noise you cannot hear the coal when it begins to stir. If this had been done in the day, and the band perhaps waiting for it, the butties will not give a man time to prick it with the long prickers, but will say, "Come, bring the band here, I see it's safe", and perhaps a piece falls and kills a man. When I worked at Hooker Hill (probably Ocker Hill) Tipton, I remember a man being killed by the band being hurried under the stuff where the roof was rotten, and a piece of rock fell on him and knocked a hole in his side. I really think if they had looked before they ordered the band in, this man's life might have been saved.

Colliery workers take a well-deserved break for this photograph at Jacko's Pit, Lower Gornal about 1919.

Often the pikemen had to jump back to avoid the falling of a mass of coal, and another of their number declared that the operation was "worse than a field of battle full of soldiers, to be forced to go to draw the coals before it's settled and made secure. And, perhaps, the doggies (foremen) will say, 'Go in, we must have these coals drawn out.'" Unhappily, accidents were as plentiful as the coal that was carved out from the pits. For every 100 working men there were 72 accidents each year. Five of these were fatal. Many others led to the breaking of limbs and the loss of work. There was no recompense for widows and disabled miners. They were hard and harsh times and if you did not work then you had no money, and if you could not earn then the only path ahead was that through the Archway of Tears and into the hated workhouse. Working people would do any job, no matter how low paid and dirty to hold back this indignity.

Many of the accidents could be laid at the feet of greedy and demanding mine owners and butties. The gaffers wanted the coal dug for as little cost as possible and competing for contracts, the butties offered prices that were as cheap as could be. This meant that not only did they drive their men on but also that they skimped on timber, candles and measures for safety. One notable exception was a butty called Mason. His pit was free of accidents and the men believed that this was because they all met at dinner time for prayers.

> About one o'clock the drink goes down the pit, and if a man is not at the place of prayer in 10 minutes after, he forfeits his drink. They sing and pray and ask a blessing on what they are going to have, and then they sit down in the road and eat their dinner and drink their beer, and after dinner one reads out of the Scripture and explains it, and tells the others what the preacher has said about it. Sometimes they get God's spirit amongst them very much, and sometimes less so. No man was allowed to join in the singing and praying unless he was thought to be living as a man should be.

In 1866 Queen Victoria came to Wolverhampton and a great arch of coal was put up in her honour and beneath which was driven her carriage. Perhaps it is time that a great arch of coal should be put up once again in the Black Country, this time to honour the Black Country miners who endured "the hardest work under heaven". Hidden from the light of day, these men steadfastly held on to their dignity and respect. They did not forget the need "to be living as a man should be" and we should not forget either them or their travails.

I should like to thank Jill Newton Richards of Heather Drive, Kinver for kindly sending me a most helpful account of Coal from the Cyclopaedia of Useful Arts and Manufacture edited by Charles Tomlinson, about 1852.

Chapter 4

DIGGING INTO THE PAST FOR
THE LIFE FORCE OF THE REGION

A vainglorious poetical wit and a scholar of renown, John Leland was probably the best-travelled man in England during the reign of Henry VII. He traipsed and rode across the kingdom, recording what he saw and giving us the earliest descriptions of most of our towns and cities. Still as energetic and keen a trecker as he was, Leland did not cover all the land and one of the areas he passed by was the northern tip of Worcestershire and the greater part of Staffordshire. Mind you, Leland was aware of places within that district. In particular, he noted the mineral resources of Staffordshire, pointing out that coal was found at Wednesbury and Walsall. And when he passed through Birmingham, the resolute traveller mentioned that a great part of the town's livelihood derived from its smiths and that they received their iron and coal from Staffordshire.

Some people suggest that there was coal mining in the county as far back as Roman times in the first centuries AD, but the first record for the activity in what was to become the Black Country dates to 1273 and relates to Sedgley. Another early working was that at the Foxyards, near to the Wren's nest, Dudley, where the Ten Yard Seam could also be dug in open workings. Within a few years, coalworking was in evidence at Kingswinford, Halesowen, Walsall and Rushall, and by 1325, coal was taken out from land in Bradley, Wednesbury, Willenhall and a spot called 'le Hyeschute' near Wednesfield. Towards the end of the fourteenth century and turn of the fifteenth century, it is apparent that coal was also got at Amblecote and Bilston.

The extraction of coal in these places was from flat mines, whereby "the workmen rid off the earth and dig the coal under their feet and carry it out on wheelbarrows". Such workings were apparent in and around Wednesbury until the late seventeenth century, and they tended to operate as small-scale undertakings – given the small population not only of South Staffordshire but also of Birmingham and the fact that wood remained the main source of fuel. But a dramatic change took place in Staffordshire in the mid-sixteenth century, so that coal was used for most household purposes "even to the parlour and bedchamber", whilst it was also the dominant fuel in a host of manufacturing processes, such as in the making of nails, locks, bricks, glass and steel.

Flat mines on the outcrop could not cater for this spectacular growth in the use of coal in the district between Wolverhampton and Birmingham and more extensive mining operations became essential to meet the demand. Often an adit, a horizontal passage, was driven into a hillside so that the coal seam could be reached. Other pits were sunk into the ground at depths generally of between eight and twenty yards, although some reached 40 yards into the earth. Of course, the deeper the pit was sunk the more likely was the need of freeing it from water. In a hill-side working, the water was drained by a tunnel that led to the lower part of the seam, whilst in other pits the water was taken away by engines with buckets or barrels that were worked by men or horses.

The development in coal mining was matched by a swelling in the numbers of colliers. Such men are indicated from the early 1400s in Wednesbury, and the parish registers in Tudor times recorded the baptism of children whose fathers were given as colliers and also, sadly, the deaths of such men "killed in the rydinge". With the marked increase both of miners and deeper mines, unfortunately the number of fatalities from mining also grew – as is obvious in the parish registers of Sedgley from 1658.

There was another major effect of coal mining, the development of the distinctive Black Country landscape. In 1739, the physician and scholar Dr John Wilkes was based in Willenhall and he depicted the gloomy vista around Wednesbury. He told of how the waste coal, or gob, burned as long as the air reached it, but went out of itself when it came to the solid wall of coal.

This evening, as I rode over part of the field where this fire was burning many acres together, the air being calm, and the weather being dry for about a fortnight, I saw on the surface of the ground, where the smoke issued out of the earth, as fine flowers of brimstone as could be made by art. They seemed to lie a handful or two in a place, but there was no possibility of going to them.

Beech Tree Colliery, Cradley which was left deserted back in 1958 – following the announcement that it was to be closed.

The black of smoke and coal, the red of fire – these were the forces that would shape the look and feel of the Black Country.

Within a generation of Wilkes's description, those forces were strengthening their grip as they captured more and more of the countryside for industry, banishing the green wherever possible. The catalyst for industrial domination and the spectacular sinking of mines was the replacement of charcoal with coal in the smelting of iron and also the cutting of canals. Iron working insatiably ate up coal, and at just the Bradley works of John Wilkinson the enormous amount of 800 tons of coal a week was needed.

By the early years of the nineteenth century it was thought that between 500,000 and one million tons of coal were burned annually in the works and furnaces of the Black Country, whilst the canals could carry the coal cheaply to a Birmingham whose population was exploding and whose metal workers were as eager for the fuel as were the ironmasters of South Staffordshire. Between ten and fifteen miles was the maximum distance over which coal could be shifted profitably on the roads of seventeenth and eighteenth century England. Birmingham was within that distance of the South Staffordshire coalfield but the passage was expensive and slow. The Birmingham Canal broke through that barrier of cost and time, so much so that on the day in 1769 that coal from Wednesbury first reached Birmingham by canal its price almost halved per hundred weight.

It's 1967 and even as the tower blocks go up in Brierley Hill the earth is torn apart for open-cast mining, leaving the familiar black, lunar landscape.

*Carols were sung hundreds of feet underground at Lower Gornal Colliery in the run-up to Christmas in 1952. The Reverend R. M. Timms, vicar of Lower Gornal, and the Reverend G. F. Hunt, Methodist minister of the area, conducted a carol service with the miners during their mid-shift for their snap. Young **Hannah Jeavons** aged twelve of **Wallows Wood, Lower Gornal** was delighted to see this photo because the older members of her family told her that the man seated second from right is her great grandfather, Victor Hickman.*

By 1837, output of coal in the Black Country exceeded 2 million tons annually and with the coming of the railways the digging of coal was given further momentum. The ravenous need for coal led to the working out of shallower pits and the necessity of sinking ever deeper below ground. In 1710 a depth of 180 feet had been reached at a pit west of Dudley. Unsurprisingly this meant that new methods were required to fetch out the water and prevent flooding. This led to the use of Newcomen's steam engines to raise the water. In 1712 at a site near Dudley Castle, Newcomen erected his first machine, and it was also the first workable engine in the world to have a piston and cylinder. A full-scale replica of a Newcomen Engine is on display at the Black Country Living Museum.

So astonishing was the success of Newcomen's first machine that the Spanish ambassador left London in great state and with a large train to see the marvel – and, more importantly, to try and catch hold of its workings so that they could be employed in Spain. He arrived at Dudley Castle but was not allowed to enter the engine house, even though he was flashing around money to try and gain access. Successfully deterred from his purpose by the folk of the Black Country, he went back to London "in a bad temper, without having a chance of seeing more than the wonderful effect this small engine was able to produce".

From the Soho Foundry, Smethwick, James Watt further improved the efficiency of steam engines and so allowed colliers to dig ever deeper for coal. Towards the end of the eighteenth century pits at Bloomfield and Wednesbury were prospected as much as 300 feet and more down, but by now the ascendancy of the latter town in Black Country coal mining was waning. Instead Bilston, Dudley, Coseley, Sedgley and Tipton were taking centre stage.

Frederick Hackwood, an indefatigable historian of the Black Country, declared "that the glory of Tipton has been its wonderful resources in coal and iron". Indeed in 1851, a massive piece of coal from Tipton was exhibited at the Great Exhibition in London. Weighing six tons, it was cut into a cylindrical shape six feet across by six feet high, whilst its surface was polished so smooth that it was like jet.

Within a few years, West Bromwich and Rowley Regis burst through as the major centres of coal production in the Black Country. In 1800 there were no pits in Bramich as it was spoken locally, but by 1832 there were 58. Similarly, by 1854 there were thirteen collieries in Rowley parish. Over the next few decades coal

A Black Country collier holing for coal in the South Staffordshire coalfield.

A historic day over half a century ago, as the last pit pony is brought to the surface at the Coombs Wood Colliery, Cradley on May 31st 1952.

mining activity then increased in the south west of the Black Country. Further north, drainage problems and the working out of the best seams led to a decline in the number of pits, but those of the Stour Valley were invigorated by the cutting of the Netherton Tunnel in the 1850s. This was the third and biggest cut linking the Stour Valley collieries with the well developed industrial district to the north and east of the Rowley Hills.

Such an expansion ensured that output from the Black Country coalfield continued to rise so that by 1870 it was more than eight million tons a year. However, long-term contraction now beckoned. There were few places left in which to sink mines. New supplies were evident in Tividale, but this was limited in its prospect, whilst flooding threatened many other pits. For a few years in the 1870s, a boom in iron and steel production masked the problems facing the Black Country mining industry. Stimulated by demand, abandoned pits were re-opened, more miners were taken on and a mines drainage scheme was implemented. For all this, output went up only marginally to nine million tons per year in 1872 and employment peaked at 28,000 men.

Seeking to maintain production, mine owners looked to the edges of the South Staffordshire coalfield. In 1874, a mine was sunk through the layer of basalt at Lye Cross and another was sunk beyond the Eastern Boundary Fault in Sandwell Park. Thanks to the initiative and skills of Henry Johnson, this mine went down 1,254 feet to reach the Thick Coal of the Ten Yard Seam. This successful operation encouraged sinkings through the sandstone to the east at Hamstead, begun in 1875 and finished five years later, and to the west at Baggeridge in 1912.

Still, the smaller and less productive pits continued to close. In 1900 there were just 276 mines in the Black Country. Only eleven employed more than 100 men underground and the biggest was that of the Earl of Dudley at Himley where 700 men laboured. The number of pits declined each year thereafter so that by 1925 – apart from Sandwell Park and Hamstead – there was just one small pit to the north of the Rowley Hills. South of that boundary there were a cluster of equally small pits around Brierley Hill and Stourbridge, each giving work to less than 50 men, and other than Baggeridge there were just two pits of any real size – at Beech Tree and Coombs Wood.

The last shift at Baggeridge Colliery in 1968. Tom Wood emerges from the cage he first went down in 1931.

Beach Tree, Halesowen employed 110 men underground and 24 on the surface and each week was raising about 5,000 tons of coal and fire clay. As opposed to the holing method that had characterised most mining in the Black Country, the Longwall method was used at Beech Tree. According to the Iron and Coal Trades Review this process meant that two roads were driven into the coal boundary to form blocks 50 yards by 40 yards. Coal was brought back in the retreating method.

The slipper is taken out first and the upper measures taken down consecutively. The dirt bands here are useful, as they provide building up materials for the men to get the upper measures in the wastes, each measure forming a small face on its own. The coal is "backened" down "bolt holes" to the tubs. The thinner seams also on longwall retreating are, of course, worked off first. It will be understood that the coal is all hand-got. The men work on a tonnage basis, fire their own shots, using ordinary black powder.

Beach Tree was closed in the late 1950s.

Coombs Wood, Cradley, belonging to the famous Hingleys of Netherton, was also opened in the early twentieth century. In 1929 it was the site of a terrible underground fire. Nine miners were cut off. One of them dared to escape through the fire and was fortunate to make it to safety, but unhappily the other eight were killed by the thick smoke and fumes as they awaited rescue. They were John Hargreaves of Smethwick, John Westwood of Darby End, George Parkes of Blackheath, Edward Barnsley of Old Hill, Edward Dukes of The Lye, Joseph Chance of Wollascote; James Harris of Netherton, and Harry Edwards of Old Hill. Seven of the men left widows, four left behind children mostly at work, whilst Edward Dukes left a young widow who was pregnant. The pit was closed in 1952.

By this date the South Staffordshire coalfield was dying. There was some open cast mining around Wolverhampton and a few small pits in other spots, but production was centred on Hamstead, Sandwell Park and Baggeridge. Today all three are closed and mining has all but disappeared from the Black Country. But if the mines and colliers are gone, the changes they wrought in the landscape are still marked by the name the Black Country whilst the endeavours of the miners themselves should always be held fast in our minds because of their essential contribution to the making of modern England.

Chapter 5

MINING MEMORIES

Harry Oliver of Leighswood Avenue, **Aldridge** was stirred to write to me by a photo of Baggeridge Colliery in the Black Country Memories column as he worked there as an apprentice electrician for three-four years "and finished my time there. I was working on the surface with an old electrician called Frank Baugh. When a lorryload of drill machines and other equipment came in from area workshops, we had to check every stone-drill machine, which ran at a lower rate of revs than the ordinary coal ones. Baughie said to me 'Get the book to write the numbers in the designated columns'. So he was rhyming numbers off and I'm writing in the book. When he finished he asked to check the book and he was not impressed! He asks why every set of numbers end in an 8? I said it was what he was saying and he straight away hit me over the head with a solid piece of cable. Every time he said the number he finished with 'eay it'. Me from the North East of England and him from Gornal – need I say more!

"Every 'snap-time' in workshops, Frankie Guest would open his sandwiches and Pat Timmins would ask him what he'd got. And it was always the same answer – bung-hole. Very thick bread with equally thick cheese which he shoved under a grill. It smelt divine. But every day he would have the same – even having a look to see if it had changed. Year in, year out – and Timmins would still ask – every god-

A drawing by Arthur Arrowsmith of Brereton Pit and the Staffordshire land surrounding it.

darn day. When I was at Littleton Colliery, Cannock, there was a haulage supply operative called 'Tiger' from Featherstone way – cause he was always on about the red, white and blue. Very good at his job, thinking of it he was fantastic. He never let anyone down – you asked him for it and he would tell you when. He was getting machinery off this one district and the worst thing happened – his haulage rope broke. It snapped due to too much load, as ever. Not to be outdone, he still got the machinery out by the end of the shift. The under-manager questioned him, 'How on earth could you get the stuff out with the rope broke?' Tiger said, 'I had to tie a knot in it'. This is three quarters inch thick steel stranded rope.

"Another day I was working in a heading with a great big 'boring' machine. One deputy, one electrician, one fitter, 4-6 big hitters (who were the headers). We were all unloading a supply car of boards, apart from the deputy, who was sitting there. One of the blokes threw a board down quick, when he saw a b... great big spider. Everybody laughed at him jumping back so quick, but the deputy kept on shouting 'Kill it! Kill it!' And when everybody was trying to get the spider, the deputy said, 'We don't want anything that fast down here'.

"Another one. A bloke who was cross-eyed – called 'cod-eye' – forgot his bait. So he phoned from down the pit to his missis to bring it to the pit. She did – and it got down the pit by-an-by. When he opened it he said it wasn't his. He was holding jam and bread, and he had put up cheese and bacon. Some entrepreneur had exchanged it along the route. The same cod-eye was breaking big-uns on a chain conveyor when he caught the signal wire I had just put up. The wire allows anyone to stop the chain anytime, hanging about six feet high along the length of the conveyor. His hammer caught the wire – when the tension of the wire being pulled down, pulled back his hammer, hit his head and knocked him out. When I said cod-eye was down, someone shouted, 'Have a look and see if it's straightened his eye out'.

"First aid down the pit. A bloke broke his leg – the first aiders gathered around and put his leg in a

Through the mist. Hamstead Colliery in the early twentieth century.

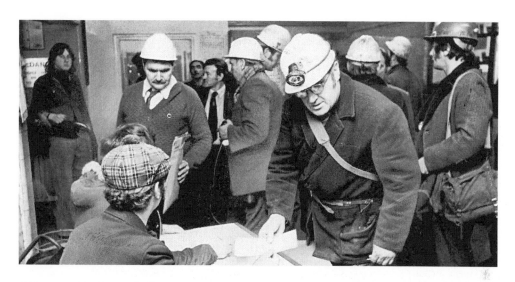

Miners at Littleton Colliery who took part in a national ballot on retirement ages in December 1976.

splint. They got the stretcher ready but when they tried to pick him up they had fastened his leg to the haulage rope as well! By the way, did you know that at Baggeridge the shaft at the bottom had a bend in it? It's the only one I have ever known, and the engineman on the surface could not get up the speed until he had cleared the bend."

As a vet, Douglas Franklin of Saint George's Parade, **Wolverhampton** used to treat a pit pony "somewhere in the Sedgley-Gornal area, down a 'Driffit' – a cave-like opening in the earth, reached by a small metal truck on a rail and operated by simple winding gear at the entrance. My last visit sometime between 1946 and 1956 was to see the pony with colic (belly ache). I crouched down in one truck and my minder in another. We travelled slowly for probably ten minutes. Messages were passed by my 'fellow traveller', touching two wires, making a contact. We stopped and there was the pony, on a cut-out 'stable' in the coal face. Not sure of illumination, perhaps a lantern? I think there was a possibility of candles as well – probably not much whiff of methane in a drift! Could have been electricity, just not sure. The poor pony was in pain. I injected some morphine and administered a colic draught by stomach tube – up a nostril and right into the stomach. Then the slow, tumbling journey out of the cold blackness back to daylight. I revisited the drift later in the day and all was well. The pony was munching hay and was quite content."

Alan Beach of Southerdown Road, **Sedgley** came on my BBC WM a few years back to talk about a copy of a map of The Coppice and Hurst Hill that was drawn about 1930 by his brother. His son, Ian, although living in Western Australia holds

A machine used at Littleton Colliery in the Longwall Retreat System to make new tunnels at the pit in the 1960s.

fast to his Black Country roots and has put together a cracking website on the Ancient Manor of Sedgley, www.sedgleymanor.com. It covers the old hamlets of Sedgley, Coseley, Upper and Lower Gornal, Gospel End, Woodsetton, Cotwall End, Ettingshall and Brierley (now called Bradley), and has sections on People, Surname Research; Churches and Chapel; Black Country Dialect; Censuses; Trades Directories; Photos; and Historical Research – amongst others.

Ian's dad, Alan, has kindly sent me a copy of a map showing some of the mines in the Sedgley area. It is called 'Staffordshire Sheet LXVII-3 – First Edition 1884' and is a fascinating document that emphasises just how pitted was the Black Country with working and abandoned collieries. Between Rookery Hall and Hurst Hill, lay the disused Rookery Colliery. The map indicates 26 old, in use or air shafts. To the other side of Ettingshall Lane and Rookery Road were Ettingshall Colliery and Spring Hill Colliery. Another 37 shafts of various kinds were to be found in this area. Between Upper Ettingshall and Deepfields were to be found Priory Fields Colliery and Breen Rhydding Colliery dotted about with 22 types of shaft. Finally, across the Stour Valley Railway were the Deepfields Colliery and Ladymoor Colliery.

A while ago Richard Hargreaves of Woodfield Avenue, **Pensnett** contacted me as he was searching for the exact position of the Dandy Mine in Pensnett. This is not shown on the Ordnance Survey Maps of 1882, 1903, 1919 and 1937, although there is a Dandy Bank Road on the Pensnett Trading Estate. Richard's interest was aroused because he is a collector of postcards and has one showing a church parade passing through High Street and Commonside towards High Oak. He was told that this event commemorated the four men who lost their lives in the Dandy Mine Disaster on 21 April 1923.

On that day, 57 miners were working in the pit when some of the miners became concerned at the amount of water that was seeping into the mine. About mid-day there was a terrific flood of water and the colliers ran as fast as they could to shift. Most made it to the surface, but when a roll call was made it was found that five men were missing. They were Ernie Haydon, a 40 year old married chap from Wordsley; William Simmons, another married man from Pensnett; Job Dando, also married from Bromley; and Tom Jordan of Coopers Bank and Enoch Cadman of Kingswinford, both of whom were single. These men had been working towards uncharted, old tunnels that no-one had been near for decades, although Enoch Cadman may have been in a position to reach higher ground. Rescue workers set to with pumping equipment, but made little impact upon the depth of the water. As in all mining communities, an accident down the pit drew everyone together in a show of solidarity and communal support. People lined the nearby streets, hoping for good news.

At last a rescue team was able to make its way down the shaft. They located a live pit pony but found their way blocked by a tub wedged in the tunnel to the pit. Two days later, the rescuers found Enoch Cadman alive, sitting on a ventilation passage on the way to the thick coal. He was with four other pit ponies still alive. He had been in the dark for 48 hours and he was clammed and worn out from trying to scramble out. When he saw the man who found him, Enoch exclaimed, "Yo must be an angel, but yo've bin a long time a comin." Unhappily, the four other men were found dead lower down. They had no chance of escaping the rush of water. Again as was customary in pit villages, a collection was launched for the dependants of the men and the mine owners paid for the funerals. Thousands turned out to pay their respects when the men were buried in Wordsley Parish Church and Pensnett Parish Church.

In pursuit of his research, Richard came across two poems about the disaster. This was a common thing after a tragedy of any kind and followed on from the traditions of the ballad singers and sellers of sheets of ballads in the nineteenth century. One was written by a Mr Campbell, late of the 1st Royal Warwicks. He writes poignantly of how the water "screamed through this cruel death-trap hole, tearing on like a roar of thunder", and of how when the new spread "Men, women and children rushed to the pit head, crying, weeping, children squealing, for their loved ones who were lying dead". The other poem is also full of pathos. It was written by William Adams of New John Street, Blackheath and was headed "A few lines of reference to the ill fated Miners: William Simmons, Thomas Jordan, Ernest Haden, Job Dando who met their fate through that sad catastrophe at the Dandy Pit, Shut End, Pensnett, on Saturday April 21st 1923 resulting in the loss of four precious lives".

In the dark regions of the earth,
  The Miner plods his way;
Facing the task so difficult,
  To gain his weekly pay.

When once he steps into the cage,
  His life again on a thread!
The signal's given and down he goes,
  Not knowing what's ahead.

Those pretty rays of sunshine,
  All lost to him by sight;
He uses lamp or candle,
  For artificial light.

Out step the little Ponies,
  From caves cut in the rock!
Longside their nippy drivers,
  To toil till lillycock.

Hush! What is that noise roaring?
  It reaches one and all;
The pounded water bursted –
  Whatever will befall?

Study the feelings of these men,
  When all their light was gone!
But, thank the Lord, the Hostler came
  And led them with his one.

The icy hand of fate was there,
  Claiming the other four;
No hope of rescue anywhere,
  It proved their bolted door.

Death visited those little homes,
  That once were bright and gay;
And took their loved one from the spot
  For ever and for aye.

(To sacrifice a little time
  Each day for fervent prayer;
God's love entwine beneath the mine,
  To keep them in his care.

The seed would grow His truth to show,
  And ripen after bloom;
Jesus to know is heaven below,
  The one faithful Bridegroom.)

Farewell dear wives, now do not mourn,
  Although your loss is great;
Our race is run, – the water won,
  Too awful to relate.

Oh, how they miss their father's hand,
  Returning home from toil;
That grip of love, light as the dove,
  And sweet refreshing smile.

How sad it seems now in the homestead,
  Those footsteps no longer we hear.
No father or husband to guide us,
  Their sweet loving words did us cheer.

Although they are gone, – not forgotten,
  So long on this earth we do dwell;
And trusting to meet them in Heaven,
  Emmanuel's chorus to swell.

Now that coal mining has disappeared from the Black Country, should we not remember those men in the Dandy Pit disaster by putting up a memorial to them close to the former colliery?

Chapter 6

A MURDEROUS TRADE FOR WHITE SLAVES OF ENGLAND

It was a sight that seared itself into his soul as much as into his mind. Here in Cradley Heath, in the heart of one of the wealthiest countries in the world, the journalist and social campaigner Robert Sherard, watched as a mother strove to earn the vital shillings she needed to stave off starvation for her and her baby. A spike maker, she laboured on her own in a shed fitted with a forge and anvil – on her own bar for her child who sat in a tiny swing chair that dangled from a pole that ran across the workshop. That way the woman could grind away whilst she still minded her babby.

The previous week she and her husband had turned a ton of iron into spikes. For this hard graft they had brought in the meagre sum of twenty shillings between the pair of them. Out of this they had paid 3s 8d (18 pence) for breeze, fuel, and the same amount for the rent of their home and workshop. On top of that they had been forced to spend one shilling to attend to damaged tools. That left them with just over eleven shillings (55 pence) to raise their family of five children. This was at a time when the poverty line was put at round about a pound a week for a moderate family. Worn out from slogging away, she was just able to ward off destitution and the break up of her family.

The son of a clergyman, Sherard had looked upon many a scene of harsh and ill-paid collar in his travels across England. Disturbed and angered by the privations of the nailers of Bromsgrove and of exploited workers elsewhere in the country, he was determined to draw attention to "the worst-paid and most murderous trades of England". He did so in 1896 in a series of articles for Pearson's Magazine. Collectively these forceful, unsettling and challenging pieces were called *The White Slaves of England*.

Sadly, Cradley Heath, Old Hill, Cradley and the locality fell firmly within Sherard's remit. There was much that was harrowing in the district, especially amongst its chainmakers. Sherard noted that the industry had never been so prosperous, at least if the amount of chain produced and workers employed were indications of well being. Each week Black Country chaps and wenches made 1,000 tons of chain – chains of every kind that you could think of, from massive four inch mooring cables down to Number 16 on the wire gauge and including rigging chains, crane cables, mining cables, cart and plough traces, curbs, halters, cow ties, dog chains and even handcuff links.

In a moving and ironic observation, Sherard declared that "if chains for slaves are not made here also it is doubtless because there are no slaves in England; or it may be because hunger can bind tighter than any iron links. And chronic hunger is the experience of most of the women workers in Cradley Heath". One woman chainmaker told him that "We has to do with two quartern (four pound) loaves a day, though three such loaves wouldn't be too much for us." With a husband and six children, this woman had been out of work since Christmas and she detailed to Sherard how she managed to get by with little money coming in. When possible she bought a pennyworth of bits of bacon, two-pennyworth of meat from the "chep butcher" and a pennyworth of potatoes, which she cooked up to make a dinner for eight. But too often they were clammed, making do with dripping begged "off them as belongs to me" to spread on a piece.

Dick Bloomer, left, a chainmaker since the age of twelve forges yet another link for his latest piece of chain with his nephew, Robert Bloomer, in this photograph taken in 1974. The men were both directors of Noah Bloomer and Sons Ltd, chainmakers which were based in Quarry Bank.

Milk was a luxury that was beyond the reach of this woman battling to keep her family together and struggling to feed them. And as for her children and milk, they had to do without it "the same as we". Like so many youngsters throughout the Black Country, the children were weaned on sop – a mashed up meal made from the drippings of the tea pot and extra hot water poured on to stale bread. In a good week, a bit of margarine might be bought and each week this determined and resourceful mother scraped together enough cash to buy a quarter of tea at a shilling a pound and four pounds of sugar at three ha'pence. As for eggs well, "I'd like one for my tea. I haven't had one for years."

Clothing was secondhand, the cast offs of those who were more fortunately circumstanced. The mother herself wore a pair of men's high-low boots, and none of her family had more "nor he stood up in". When the children's stockings were washed, the youngsters had to be put to bed because none of them "had one bit to his feet". As part of her daily struggle to resist the waves of poverty and to remain independent and clean, this woman did her washing on a Saturday night after she had finished work. No truer words were spoken than that working-class women worked all their lives.

This particular Black Country wench made heavy chain at 5s 4d for a hundredweight (one twentieth of a ton). If she laboured continually for twelve hours a day she could make about one and a half hundredweight a week. But at what a cost to her body and soul was that inadequate and insulting sum earned! Her hands were blistered badly and she was burnt all over her body from the sparks that flew from her hammering of the metal. Yet this woman was not bowed down nor broken by her adversities. She remained cheerful, explaining "It's not what I gets to eat. It's me having a contented mind, and not letting nothing trouble me."

Deeply affected by the dignity and doggedness of this woman of the Black Country, Sherard could not forget her. After he left Cradley Heath and returned to his home in Ambleside, he sent her a basket of eggs. In return, the woman went to great lengths to send her thanks. She did so by way of a Scots woman who was able to read and write and who was involved, along with her father, in a Bread and Tea Fund that provided help for families in Cradley Heath in the winter. The letter of thanks went:

> I beg to thank you for the box of eggs, which came to hand quite safely, and which myself and husband and children thoroughly enjoyed. It was quite a treat for us to have such a thing in our house. The young lady who is writing this letter for me knows how hard I have had to work to make an honest living. There is eight of us in the family, and only my second son, a boy of thirteen years of age, getting 4s a week for blowing in a chainmaker's shop, and myself, who makes chain; and after working hard from 7 a.m. till 9 p.m., from Monday till dinner-time Saturday, and receive 6s.

Making his way through Cradley Heath, Sherard saw many workshops where five or six women worked at the anvil, talking above the "the din of their hammers and the clanking of their chains, or they may be singing a discordant chorus". Outsiders could be lulled by this sociability into missing the deep signs of want – the old clothes worn by the women, their haggard faces and the pinched looks of their infants. So needy were the women for their sparse wages that they worked throughout their pregnancies. In a matter-of-fact way, one female chainmaker described how, on the day that her son was born, she collared at making chain-harrows – for five shillings (25p) a week – up till five in the afternoon, "and then I give over because I had my cleaning to do". The baby was born less than two hours after she packed in her paid labour for that of making sure her home was spotless.

Once delivered, the baby was usually cared for within the workshop, so that the mother could carry on chainmaking. It cost 2s 3d (13 pence) to pay someone to mind a child and this was an expense that could not be borne, as was made plain by a woman whose eyes reminded Sherard of Leah, the first wife of Jacob in the Book of Genesis and who was the mother of six sons. Over three days she had forged 728 heavy links, receiving two shillings and tuppence (11p). Out of this she had to pay seven pence ha'penny (3p) for firing, and if she had paid a nurse one shilling (5p) she would have been left with just sixpence ha'penny (2½p) for all her toil and moil. The Leah-like mother had no doubt about how she and her people were treated, "We'm working worse nor slaves, and getting nothing to eat in the bargain".

Chainmakers at Noah Hingley's, Netherton, 1911.

Like all chainmakers, the women workers heated iron rods – pulling the bellows for each link – then bent the red hot piece, cut it in on the hardy, twisted the link, inserted it into the previous link on the chain and welded or closed it with repeated blows of the hand hammer and the bigger Oliver hammer that was worked by a treadle. Female chainmakers mostly worked in small workshops or at the back of their own homes and made the lighter chain, although within the bigger factories where men made the heavy chain the bellows were tended by women and girls.

Sherard was deeply upset by seeing "a sweet little lass – such as Sir John Millias (a famed artist) would have liked to paint – dancing on a pair of bellows for 3d a day to supply 'blast' to the chainmaker of the forge, and to put 3d a day into the pockets of her employer. As she danced her golden hair flew out, and the fiery sparks which showered upon her head reminded me of fire-flies seen at night near Florence, dancing over a field of ripe wheat." The young girl was one of many ensnared by the sweaters. These were men who were engaged to provide labour for the factories and who beat down the wages they paid so that they might gain more from the difference between the money paid across by the gaffer and that actually received by the worker. Decried by Sherard as a misuser of children, the man who sweated "the sweet little lass" was declaimed as "the most reprehensible thing that offends" in the district. Unhappily, he was not on his own. Sweaters abounded locally, preying upon the working poor, forcing them to labour for low wages in unsafe, dirty and rough conditions.

It was through apprenticeship indentures that many of these sweaters chained the chainmaking young to a life of bound labour. One such indenture referred to a girl of fourteen. She was supposedly apprenticed to the arts and trade of chainmaking but in reality she was another source of cheap labour, for she was paid but 2s 6d (12½p) a week. Sherard believed that she was actually little more than ten years old. He had never before seen such little arms, "and her hands were made to cradle dolls". Instead they were forced to make links for chain harrows, whilst another "female wisp" besides her was forging dog chains. With the swivel and ring complete, this earned her the hopeless amount of three farthings (three quarters of a penny). The chain itself sold for 1s 6d (7½p). Working for ten hours a day the poor little thing could manage six chains a day.

But it was not just men who were the sweaters. Those women who worked in workshops or at the back of their own homes had their jobs from foggers, or middlewomen. One old fogger employed seven girls in her shed. She had never forged a link of chain in her life but got a good living from the young wenches who worked for her. For each hundredweight of chain produced, this fogger was paid 5s 4d (26p), but she only passed 2s 10d (14p) on to her workers. The Chainmakers Union was fighting for a level of 4s for the workers, allowing the still swollen profit of 25% to the fogger. Sherard damned this fogger "as one of a numerous class of leeches fast to a gangrened sore".

The female chainmakers did not suffer their vile conditions and mistreatment without fighting back. In his wonderful account of growing up in Cradley, the highly-respected Cliff Willetts stressed that "these women were as hard and as durable as the chains they made. They had to be, to endure the conditions in which they lived." Many of them were devout Methodists and sang the hymns sung by Sankey, the American evangelist who had visited England twice. And from their number arose trade unionists avowed to improve the lot of their fellows.

In 1908 a woman's branch of the Cradley Heath Hammered Chainmakers joined the National Federation of Women Workers and a year later the trade unionists gained a small success when the new Trades Boards fixed a minimum wage of 2½d an hour for chainmakers in Cradley, Cradley Heath and Old Hill. The next year, the female chainmakers joined an outpouring of activity by women workers. A number of employers had prevailed upon their workers to contract out of the agreement for a minimum wage for a period of six months. It was feared that the gaffers would use this time to build up stocks of chain so that when the minimum wage did come into force they would be able to lay off their workers. In effect, the chainmakers would be punished by unemployment for combining to protect themselves.

The Federation recommended that those women who had signed should cancel their action and that those who had not signed should remain resolute. Faced by such steadfastness the more responsible employers of the Manufacturers' Association agreed to pay their workers the minimum wage so long as these chainmakers financially supported those women who refused to sign the agreement and who worked for bosses not part of the Association. The women trade unionists of Cradley Heath and district bravely took on this hard task. A public appeal was launched to raise money and nearly £4,000 was collected quickly. Bolstered by this fund, the female chainmakers were able to help their fellows who were locked out by the sweaters – and they were able to fight to the finish. After thirteen weeks they returned to work victorious – for every employer in the area had signed up to the agreement. By 1914, the chainmakers were now earning 12s 4½d a week. It was still too little but it was almost double the sum before the Federation began its campaign of unionisation.

The Workers Institute on the corner of Lower High Street and Whitehall Road was built with the money left over from the strike fund. It was a centre locally for female trade unionism and became the headquarters of the Chainmakers and Strikers Association until 1972. It is now to be taken down brick by brick and put up again at the Black Country Living Museum. Its presence will be a lasting and fitting tribute to hard-working women who bettered their own working conditions through their own endeavours and in so doing inspired countless thousands more.

Mary Macarthur, leader of the National Federation of Women Workers, addressing chainmakers at Four Ways, Cradley Heath during the lock out of 1910. This photo was taken by Edwin Beech of Imperial Studios, Cradley Heath. Mary Macarthur, the champion of the female chainmakers of Cradley Heath, Cradley, Old Hill and district, is probably the woman standing on the trap in the centre. She was a woman whose championing of the poor and the marginalised has gained the admiration of Norman Jones of Stourbridge – and he has sent me a bookmark of an election leaflet handed out during the General Election of December 1918. The leaflet focused upon the needs of children and featured Mary Macarthur's daughter, Nancy.

Born in 1880, this combative and passionate campaigner for the rights of women was a Scot who played a vital role in unionising the women chainmakers. After the First World War, when some women were given the vote, she was chosen to stand as the candidate for the newly-emerging Labour Party in Stourbridge. As Norman points out, "she failed to become our first woman M.P. by a whisker, thanks to some extent due to the dirty tricks of her opponents at the election. One of the tricks was to force her to use her married name, Henderson, when she was better known and more easily recognisable as McA i.e. Macarthur." Sadly, Mary Macarthur died three years later aged just 41.

Norman Jones himself is an outstanding historian of HalesOwen and a key figure in the HalesOwen History Society. His numerous publications include a series on a story teller of genius, Billy Hackett of Hasbury, and they ensure that folk like Billy will never be forgotten. Norman has written about Mary Macarthur via

Billy's reminiscences in his book Parish Pump to Parliament (HalesOwen History Society Publication, 1992). He recites that:

> They worshipped her in Cradley. We couldn't have had a better candidate: a fine looking woman and a wonderful speaker. I'd been to two or three of her meetings at Cradley, but the first time I met her was when she turned up at our headquarters in HalesOwen. What a personality. She seemed to fill the room. She'd got a young Irish woman with her who'd come over to the country to work on munitions during the war. She'd taken on the job as Mary Macarthur's agent and she was looking for lodgings in the district. I said I should consider it a privilege if she'd come and live at our house. She did and she was with us for nearly a month. During that time she was out every day knocking on doors, trying to persuade people to vote Labour.

I salute Norman for his work in ensuring that those yet unborn shall know not also about those long gone but also shall understand their trials, tribulations, triumphs and achievements.

Now part of one of the area's best-known attractions, the Black Country Living Museum, Lench's oliver shop was originally built between 1908 and 1910. Inside the shop were made shackles, hooks, clips and fastenings and visitors to the museum can see for themselves the oliver, a spring hammer used by blacksmiths and chainmakers, in action. The museum, off the Tipton Road, attracts thousands of visitors each year with its buildings, displays and memorabilia charting the history of the Black Country.

Anthony Page from Halesowen has dropped me a thoughtful note about working at William Lench's Oliver Shop of Blackheath, which has now been transferred to the Black Country Living Museum. He began work one Monday aged 15, after leaving school the previous Friday, for a wage of £2 9s 6d (£2 47½p). One place which "I loved to visit during my job was the Oliver Shop in Ross, into which you had to go through a gate at the side of Luther Westwood's, who also worked at Lench's. The Oliver Shop stretched the length of Woodhouse Grocers, Ivy's fish shop, Hampton's Hosiery and Oldacres General Stores. To enter you would go through the top door and on the left were the offices, which were littered with orders and other paperwork covered in dust, nuts and bolts, with cobwebs everywhere.

"To the right you came to the workshop itself, that was in the same state as the office. On the beams there were bits of tools, broken pulley belts, dust and cobwebs. The windows were dirty and a pile of coke for the forge lay in the corner. It had a lot of faults but I was fascinated by it all. Two men worked there, Ezra Homer and Len Griffin, who always kept a Billy can by the forge and they would say 'tea's on, help yourself', but I always refused as it looked like treacle, having been stewing for some time. If I went down at breakfast time they would heat a bar of steel and hold it over the bacon and sausage sandwiches to warm them up. It smelled delicious.

"I would also have to go to the warehouse in High Street, Blackheath. It was a ramshackle place made of corrugated sheets and there I would see Dennis Slim. He always rode a bike to work. I saw him a few weeks ago and he still rides a bike. Sometimes while going down to High Street I would have to wait by Thomas' Butchers while they delivered cows, sheeps or pigs for slaughter. Often one would escape. I swear they knew what was coming.

"Lench's always looked after the workforce. On Saturday night there was a dance in the canteen and in the week a social club run by Percy Dudley. Saturday afternoon we would play football. Sunday there were fishing contests, all available to anyone interested."

Another Anthony Page is another historian dedicated to the passing on of the past of the place to which he belongs. In his case it is Blackheath and Anthony has brought out two important works on the town, Blackheath (Sutton Publishing, 2000) and Blackheath. A Second Selection (Sutton Publishing, 2002). He has also played a key role in the formation of a thriving local history society with distinguished members such as the talented and perceptive poet, Tossie Patrick, someone else who is rightly proud of Blackheath.

Chapter 7

PROUD WORKERS CHAINED
TO A LIFETIME OF HARD TOIL

Cliff Willetts was a Black Country mon proud of his people, their speech, their hard collar and their achievements. Bred and born in Cradley, his mother was a chainmaker. Like so many of her folk she knew only one way of living – work, family and worship. Her wedding day highlighted those constants in her life. The year was 1877 and along with a dozen other wenches she was working as a chainmaker at a chain shop on the corner of Lyde Green and Bridge Street in Cradley. At about eleven in the morning, she packed up what she was a doing. As she did so, she placed her hammer and tongs in the bosh, a cast iron kind of basin in which the tools were cooled, and she washed her hands and arms in the dark water of the bosh. After drying herself with her sweat cloth, she wiped her brow and put on her shawl, holding it together with a pin. That done, she put her flat cap on her head, also with a pin through it to keep it fixed to her hair, and she took off her chainmaker's apron and replaced it with a clean, white pinny.

Keeping on her hob-nailed boots, for she had nothing else for her feet, she told her pals she wouldn't be long and went out. An hour later she came back and showed her mates her wedding ring, explaining why she had been away so long by declaring, "Well, yo cor get married in five minutes cor yer". Cliff's mom had met her chap outside Cradley Parish Church. They had no witnesses and waited until a woman came by who was carrying flowers to place on a grave. They asked her and someone else they did not know to act as witnesses – which they did. After the wedding both bride and groom went back to work, unable to afford even a celebratory drink because they had paid all their money on the Church fees. Years later, when asked why she and her man had not even had a wedding day embrace, she answered dismissively, "We day have time for that saftness, we had to goo back ter werk". Having had an hour off for her wedding, she grafted that night till nine instead of till eight – and that was her honeymoon.

Like his mother and father, Cliff himself was born to the hammer and he was alert to the structure of the industry locally as only an insider could be. His mom worked in a shop that was just two or three steps beyond the back door. Such small workshops had one or two hearths. Nearby in Anvil Yard, Cradley the residents worked in slightly larger shops with up to three hearths. This gathering of tiny, badly-built cottages brought to the fore the exploitation of the chainmakers of the Black Country.

In 1888 the senses of an investigator for the Board of Trade were overwhelmed by the terrible conditions in Anvil Yard, later cleared to become the Memorial Gardens. This small collection of overcrowded and insanitary buildings included fourteen houses and ten chain shops. The investigator noted that "in one case, a covered drain running past the end of a dwelling house, struck damp through the house wall from floor to ceiling; open drains everywhere carrying off household refuse and ruinous privies with overflowing ashpits, loaded the atmosphere with the most pungent odours. Here also are the little domestic workshops, built on to the houses, so that the occupants can step at once from kitchen to anvil."

Almost twenty years later, Robert Sherard was so angered and distressed by the open sewers and vile environment of Anvil Yard that he brought to mind lines of Goethe, the famed German writer, to describe the lives of the folk of Cradley: "zwischen den Amboss und Hammer" – between the anvil and the hammer. Despite the terrible conditions of life in Anvil Yard, the people were God-fearing and strove to stay clean and respectable. Born in 1911,

Cradley chain maker Laurence Harris, aged 75, carries on a 100-year family tradition at the firm where he works – Griffin Woodhouse in Cradley Heath. Mr Harris of Ladysmith Road had been at the firm for 61 years since leaving school at the age of 14. At the time of the picture, Mr Harris was a part-time worker and was given a television set to mark his long service.

Ted Green grew up there and admired the real skills needed to make chain, a skill that he could never master. He recalled that the local women were mostly outworkers for Moles and Beddowes, and that each hearth had its female worker. The hearth burnt gledes, small pieces of coal that had been burned already in a glede oven until the smoke had disappeared. Next to the hearth was the wooden block, upon which the chain was hammered and to which was affixed the anvil that was used for shaping the links. (Ned Williams, *Black Country Folk at Werk*, Uralia Press, 1989).

A larger six-hearth shop is still to be seen at Mushroom Green. Restored by the Black Country Society under the knowledgeable guidance of Ron Moss and now run by the Black Country Living Museum, it was built in the mid-nineteenth century and was re-opened in 1977. The family most associated with the shop was that of William Kendrick. He ran it until 1915 and was followed by his son, Harry, who worked there until his death at the age of 80 in 1965. Until four years before he passed on, he carried on making chains – fitting forged round rings on to lengths of electrically welded chain. The tools in the Mushroom Green shop were set up under the expert eye of Clarry Johnson, a chainmaker at Noah

Cradley Heath Chainmakers about 1910 at the firm of Harry Stevens, Old Hill. Lucy Woodall worked here and when her boss, Mark Stevens, was having a clear out in his office he gave this photo to her. Lucy began work at the firm in the early 1920s and worked in the position on the left of the photo for 35 years. Trevor Woodall, Lucy's son, recalls that "Mrs Jennings and her next door neighbour, Mrs Perry, both worked for Mark Stevens and my Friday evening job was to take both of them their wages in a small brown envelope, sometimes still working at 6.30 p.m. The other two employees employed by Mr Stevens being Aunt Bella, she worked on the block next to my Mom, and the other being Mrs Thomason, and she worked at home – and not one husband between them."

Bloomer's, one of the last firms in the Black Country to fashion handmade chain. The chain shop at the Black Country Living Museum itself has two hearths from Bloomer's in Quarry Bank and also has a replica of a hearth at Cruddas in Cradley Heath.

Six-hearth shops provided the bridge between the small back-yard and brewus chain shops and the factory-style works that boasted between a dozen and two dozen hearths. Ted Green remembered that most of the men from Anvil Yard toiled in the large chain factories such as Jones and Lloyds, where big chain cables and anchors were made as well as small chain and nails and thimbles. Called the Scotia Works, the firm had begun in 1837.

The making of light chains had emerged from the trade of ironmongery for saddlers, and by 1813 there were fourteen such businesses in Walsall, supplying chains, rings, squares and all kinds of iron work for wagon and cart harnesses; whilst there were also five dog chain makers. That same year, Joseph Smith, an iron and coal master of Coseley, patented a heavier kind of chain for the raising of minerals from mines. Seven years later, Noah Hingley of Netherton made the first

Cable chain being made by John Brian Williams at Noah Bloomer and Sons Ltd, chainmakers of Quarry Bank in 1974.

chain cable, although some sources indicate this did not happen until 1824 and was the result of the innovation of the Billinghams.

Whatever the origins, by the later 1830s the manufacture of chains and chain cables had developed rapidly and it had become established in Tipton, West Bromwich and the district south west of Dudley – in Cradley Heath, Cradley, Old Hill and Netherton. By the 1860s, about 50,000 tons of chains and cables were made each year and a further 10,000 tons of iron were used to manufacture trace and other small chains that were mostly exported to America. Over 4,000 men, women and children laboured in small workshops and factories to produce this remarkable output of manufacturing endeavour.

The pronounced growth of chainmaking was stimulated by a number of factors. Chain cable began to replace rope for ship's cables from the 1820s, whilst there was an increased demand for cable in the growing number of mines locally. The Black Country was able to supply this demand because it had a plentiful supply of iron, a skilled and hard-working people, and its mills could accurately and expertly roll the iron needed for chainmaking. One of the leading firms was that of Joseph Wright and Co. of Tipton Green. In 1873 it gained contracts from the Russian and Turkish governments, and fifteen years later it was the first business locally to be awarded an Admiralty contract for a term of five years. By 1914, South Staffordshire and North Worcestershire had achieved an almost monopoly on the world's trade of ship's cables and during the First World War the industry successfully moved over into munitions work. However, hard times beckoned with the coming of peace.

The post-war depression triggered a decline in the demand for wrought chain. Over the decade from 1913, exports dropped drastically from 34,000 tons to 12,000 tons, whilst cheap foreign chain began to make inroads into the home market. The small workshops were hit hardest and the slow decline of Black Country chainmaking by hand had begun. Still, the bigger local firms continued to make their mark upon the world. Both the Queen Mary and Queen Elizabeth luxury liners were equipped with anchor cables made by Samuel Taylor and Sons of Brierley Hill. This business had grasped hold of the opportunity afforded by technology and had brought in electric welding and special purpose machinery,

The making of the chain itself was a captivating process. Each worker had a coke-breeze hearth like that of a blacksmith. The fire was blown by bellows and latterly by a fan blast. A piece of hot, wrought iron was cut to the necessary length and then, with nipple tongs, the first bend was made. Next, the metal was reheated to scarf it out, shape the ends so as to enable fire welding – whereby the link was shut. Once welded the link was turned on to the point of the bick-iron and was shaped by the use of the Tommy hammer, itself operated by a treadle.

Chain up to five eights of an inch in diameter was worked by one person, but bigger chain required more people. Depending on the size of the chain, generally there was one man who was the chainmaker and one or two who were strikers. Until the introduction of PAYE in 1944, the chainmaker was a butty, in that he contracted a price with the chain firm and himself paid the first and second hammer. A working day began early, at between five and six in the morning and was carried on until the day's quota had been achieved, usually by noon.

Cliff Willetts vividly brought to mind his first sight of the swinging of heavy hammers. In the early twentieth century his mother took him to the Beaconsfield Works in Toys Lane, Cradley where she had heard that there was a vacancy. The gaffer was Wilf Blackwell and he took them in the shop, where men were making shackles, thimbles, swivels and other types of ship's tackle. Three of them chaps were hard at work making 1½ inch diameter shackles: "Wilf Moore was the maker, Andrew Thomas and Albert Cox the strikers. I was fascinated as I watched Andrew and Albert swing those ten pound hammers. I marvelled at the amazing accuracy and precision with which those hammers responded to the physique and muscles in arm and body, with deadly accuracy."

Cliff noticed his mom chatting earnestly with Mr Blackwell. The gaffer asked Mrs Willetts if she thought that young Cliff could do Andrew's job of striking. Cliff was astounded, "I could hardly believe that I, a young teenager, was being seriously considered for a job swinging a 10lb sledge hammer. Then he turned to my mother and asked her, 'Think he can do it?' She gave a classic reply which resolved the argument by saying, 'Corse he con dew et, he was born with ommer in is ond'." Working in a trade allied to chainmaking and filled with workers imbued with the same craft, Cliff was in awe of the men who could mould and fashion a piece of iron into whatever was required. They had a genius that was unlimited. Each man could take a two inch diameter piece of iron and with only the hammer, anvil and fire could make a swivel, shackle, ring, hook or whatever. Give them a drawing and after a few moments study they could work out sizes, shapes and then make the product perfectly. Pulled to such men by their artistry and talent, Cliff averred that to have known them was a privilege and that "we shall never see their likes again".

And nor shall we see again the likes of Lucy Woodall, the last woman in this country to make chain by hand. Over a period of ten years, Ron Moss interviewed this notable woman and an account of her life is in Ned William's book on *Black Country Werk*. Born in Old Hill in 1899, Lucy left school on her thirteenth birthday and was apprenticed as a chainmaker to Horton's of Old Hill. She began by pumping the hand bellows to provide the air blast that kept the fires going in the hearth. Occasionally she went on the block to practice turning a link, bending the end of a hot iron into the shape of a U. Later she learned how to shut the link by fire welding the two open ends together to make a flat-sided oval link.

After she finished her apprenticeship, Lucy went to work at William Stevens in Brook Lane, Old Hill. Known locally as Steven Cook's, here she made chains for military horses. Thence Lucy moved on to Hollingsworth's in Meredith Street, Cradley Heath where she learned the highly skilled process of bolting swivels, which allowed greater movement of the chain. Finally, Lucy went on to Harry Stevens of Oak Street, Old Hill where she stopped for 35 years. By the 1950s she was the only woman chainmaker in the works and she watched as the male chainmakers fell from four to just two.

When Mark Stevens died, "this was a very sad day for me", and the works closed. The trade was taken on by Woodhouse and Sons of Corngreaves Road, Cradley Heath and Lucy went there to work in a small workshop with two other women and three men. These left one after another until Lucy was left on her own. She carried on doggedly making chain until the Christmas of 1973 "when the pain from arthritis in

In 1958, Elizabeth Jennings, aged 74, of Hall Street, Old Hill, was still working eight hours a day making chains by hand – a job she first began when she was 13.

my leg forced me to retire at the age of seventy three. I had been making chain for sixty years and one month." Lucy died six years later. With her went the craft of thousands of Black Country wenches who knew no other way than to work hard and provide for their families. They were women of whom we should be proud and whose names should be recorded so that those yet to come shall understand them, appreciate them and never forget them.

Writing the articles on chainmaking, waves of differing emotions swept across me. Anger at the harsh conditions in which so many of our people had to work and live in the richest nation in the world. Distress at the way in which so many of our people's lives were blighted by ill health and premature death. Respect for the way in which our people faced up to their hardships and did not succumb to them. Pride in their morals and principles and the way in which they strove to create a better world for those yet unborn. Admiration for their skills, talents and abilities, for their aptitude, inventiveness and crafts. And anger again at the way so many of our national politicians have failed to recognise the importance of manufacturing and have allowed our industrial endeavours to rust and rot. Surely one day someone must recognise that we cannot all serve, that someone somewhere has to make something. We are very good at making things in this region. Give our people the opportunity and we can continue to strike awe into observers because of our manufacturing prowess and industrial ingenuity.

I should like to pay tribute to Cliff Willetts who through his book *When I was a Boy* has ensured that the lives of his people will never be forgotten. I wished that I had met Cliff, but I was fortunate to have known his late daughter Hazel Clifton. Hazel was a woman through whose being coursed the lore and language of the Black Country. I met Hazel at a talk I gave years back and she was kind to me when I first began on BBC Radio WM. In particular, I recall one Saint George's Day when I wanted to do something to celebrate England and Englishness. For me the greatest gift we have is our language and I asked Hazel if she would come on the show to talk in and about Black Country dialect. She did so unhesitatingly. She was a kindly and learned woman, who always clung fast to the faith of her fathers and mothers. I am proud to have known her. She and her brother Barry Willetts also wrote an important historical work, *Cradley a History*, and Barry is engaged in another vital piece of research into the chapel used by his family. I would also like to pay tribute to the magnificent work carried out by Ron Moss and other members of the Black Country Society. The Black Country is fortunate to have such a committed band of people determined not to see the past swept away.

After reading about the harsh lives of the chainmakers, **Charles Ward of Pope Road, Underhill, Wolverhampton** makes an important point about working life in general. He notes that "although it is generally thought that Wolverhampton is not part of the Black Country, I remember the same conditions existing when I was born here. For instance my father and his father were blacksmiths working everyday objects, such as door hinges and door latches within a few yards of Saint John's Church. Indeed my grandmother was a blacksmith. She was well known for her skill at making and fitting the union tyres on carriage wheels."

The hard collaring chainmakers of the Black Country have inspired **Ted Shaw of Cox's Lane, Cradley Heath** to write a moving poem about the Black Country. Ted is a powerful and insightful poet and I thank him for his invaluable contributions to my BBC WM Sunday afternoon local history show.

The Birth of the Black Country
Was it only yesterday
That this land lay sweet and fair,
Until the blast of the Black Country furnace
Shattered the peaceful air.

When loud roared the chainshop Dragons
And bright shone their glowing eyes,
Numbing one's sense with clamour
While polluting the azure skies.

Spreading their scourge over sylvan fields
Marring the rural scene,
Changing this quiet hamlet
Into a crashing hammering machine.

A place where men toiled from early light
Fashioning white steel,
Bound to the glowing furnace
Until exhaustion made them reel.

Whilst the master lived in his mansion
And drove his carriage and four,
Urging his overseers
To drive the men still more.

Their families at home were starving
Begging a crust of bread,
And the men staggered home at evening
Scarce better than living dead.

Their earnings were merely a pittance
Scarce enough to keep body and soul,
And the records bore grim testimony
Of the monstrous horrible toll.

Thus the Black Country was born anew
Like the phoenix out of the fire,
Spawned by man's greed and despair
While the black smoke rose higher and higher.

But a wind of change blows across this land
And its men can be men again,
As the air grows sweeter and cleaner
With the Dragons laid in their den.

No longer the smoking monsters,
But a land of commercial towns,
Enjoying another rebirth
And their once world-wide renown.

A renown that was earned by sweat and tears
Of the men who made Black Country chain,
Whose skills have been lost with the passing years
And are remembered only in name.

There was Bloomer and Homer and Tilley
Brookes, Whitehouse, Billingham and Woodhall,
Davis and Jones and Taylor
The men of the old Black Country.

Theirs was a life of adversity
Filled with little of saving grace,
That gave its name to the Black Country
This once green rural chase.

Chapter 8

LUCY WOODALL –
BLACK COUNTRY WENCH

If men like Noah Hingley and Bill Perry the Tipton Slasher were men amongst men, then Lucy Woodall was a Black Country wench amongst Black Country wenches. Born and raised amongst a hard-collaring, skilled, dogged and resolute people, Lucy was the epitome of all those women who were as vital as their men in making the wares of the Black Country. The last chainmaker in England to make chain by hand, perhaps the last in the world, Lucy held the craft of chainmaking tight to her in her mind, spirit and body. As much as her family and her region, her trade was at the core of her being and Lucy could think no more of putting down her hammer as of putting away her loyalties to kin and place.

Born in Old Hill in 1899, she was one of seven children to Jane and James Swingler of Clyde Street. Jane made nails in her yard whilst James was a socket maker, but like so many chaps he suffered from bad health and was in and out of work. He had served his country in the Boer War but was invalided out because of ulcerated feet and every time they 'broke out' he was unable to earn money. In common with married women across the Black Country and Brummagem, the task of bringing in the funds to ensure the integrity of the family and its survival outside the hated workhouse was taken on unwaveringly by Jane. She had no option if she and her family were not to be pinched by hunger. And as well as grafting, Jane also resorted to the coping strategies adopted by so many working-class mothers.

Jane Swingler, Lucy Woodall's mother, outside her house in High Street, Old Hill in the 1930s.

Years later, her grandson, Trevor was minded by his grandmother because his Mom, Lucy, was working. On one occasion they were returning from Trevor's aunt's house and they stopped outside Old Hill Police Station/ Magistrates Court. Jane pointed to the building, saying contemptuously, "Those buggers fined me sixpence for stealing coal" – although as Trevor points out, Jane's language was "a little more colourful at the time". It was an age-old custom that local folk were allowed to pick the waste coal from the pit bonks, but that did not stop one policeman pinching Jane for it.

Lucy herself had to pick coal when she was young, "They'd let you pick the coal in them days. When the tubs come up the pits, the waste would be tipped down the bank and you'd pick the good bits out. You know, me and Our Bill always had to go and do that. On a Saturday morning we'd get up early to get a bit extra to sell to have summat to eat." Lucy remembered that a young, teenaged married chainmaker called Edith Painter sadly died when picking coal near the Lion Colliery. The bonk above her was unsafe and moved, causing the mound of slag to slide down and bury her.

Lucy Woodall and husband, John, with their son, Trevor. Sadly John died soon after this photo was taken. He was just 35.

When Lucy was little more than ten, the female chainmakers of Cradley, Cradley Heath and Old Hill rose up in indignation at their starvation wages and combined to form a union to fight for their rights. Some employers refused to accept their righteous demands and locked out the women workers. Lucy had vivid memories of these tough and determined women who demonstrated in Cradley Heath wearing their flat caps and shawls. A local song about the women stressed why they fought their bosses:

The lady chainmakers have all gone on strike.
The gaffers think they can pay what they like.
They work em so hard both by night and day,
And for it all they get such terrible pay.

Leaving Corngreaves School, Cradley when she was thirteen, Lucy was urged by Miss Bennett, her headmistress, to take up sewing because she was the best in her class at needle work. "'Oh Lucy', her used to say, 'Don't go into the chain. You're gifted with the needle'." Unheeding this advice Lucy went straight into the chain shop. Matter-of-factly she stated that "it was what I wanted and the money was needed at home. So I signed for an apprenticeship."

Lucy was taken on at Horton's chain factory in Park Street, Old Hill at 4 shillings (20p) a week. The hours were long and tiring for a young wench, twelve

Lucy having a tea break with her gaffer, Mark Stevens. This photo appeared in the Express and Star in 1950. Trevor Woodall, Lucy's son, now of Mincing Lane, **Rowley Regis**, *recalls that "Mrs Jennings and her next door neighbour, Mrs Perry, both worked for Mark Stevens and my Friday evening job was to take both of them their wages in a small brown envelope, sometimes still working at 6.30 p.m. The other two employees employed by Mr Stevens being Aunt Bella, she worked on the block next to my Mom, and the other being Mrs Thomason, and she worked at home – and not one husband between them.*

hours a day Monday to Friday and seven hours on the supposed half day of Saturday when Lucy knocked off at two. Even then there was no relaxing for she had to help her Mom black lead the grate and do the shopping. Raised to face up to trials and tribulations and to get on with it, Lucy was undaunted. As did every working-class youngster, she handed over her wages to her Mom, receiving back 2d for herself.

The harsh realities of working-class life meant that each child knew that their wages were not their own. They belonged to the family and it was their duty to let their mother have their money so that she might be better able to marshal her resources in the daily and unremitting battle against poverty. Many's the time Lucy's mom and dad had just a bit of bacon for breakfast: "there was never enough for we kids, you'd see, so we got the bread soaked in the fat and believed those who

A wonderful photo of Lucy Woodall working at the forge at Samuel Woodhouse in Cradley Heath in 1972. It was taken by Ron Moss. There is a small group of important and influential historians of the Black Country. Ron is one of them. The author of books on Cradley Heath, Old Hill and district, chairman of the Industrial Group of the Black Country Society, a key figure in the preserved chainshop at Mushroom Green and an advisor for the Black Country Living Museum, Ron has written the definitive book on chainmaking. It is called Chainmaking in the Black Country (Blakemore Publications). I pay tribute to Ron's invaluable work.

told us that this was the best way to keep out the cold. At work I would manage at dinner time with a sandwich of potato spread on margarine – me brother Bill had the same and it was toast and marge at tea time."

In the chainshop, Lucy slowly learned her trade. She'd work on one piece until the time was up and then move on to something else. Sometimes she would blow the bellows for the men workers and then sweep the floor or clean the toilets. Working on a bit of this and a bit of that she picked up the chainmaker's skills, chivvied along by the older workers who'd order her, "Don't do that. Don't hold yer wrist like that. Yoh'll never mek a chainmeker as long as yer wrist's stiff."

After six months, Lucy's wages went up by one and a tanner (7½p) and at the end of her first year she was put on stint work. The stint was an amount of chain she had to make in a day – and she could not go home until she had reached her target. Mind you, Lucy did not have to work over to finish her stint. Talented and industrious, she had usually accomplished what was set her before the working day was out, allowing her to do extra work. At the end of the week this additional chain was weighed and payment would be made by the piece. This much-needed sum could be as much as two bob or half a crown "and you were in heaven then. That was a fortune in them days."

After finishing her apprenticeship in 1915, Lucy moved on to Elizabeth Perry's chain shop, where she and her fellows made cavalry chain for the war effort. By now she and her family were living in High Street, Old Hill – today called Highgate Street in a perverse change by the authorities. She lived there for the rest of her life. After two years she packed it in at Perry's and went to the factory of William Stevens in Brook Lane, where there were 26 working in just one shop. Then in the early 1920s she settled down with the firm of Harry Stevens in Oak Street, Old Hill. Lucy was to work here for 35 years.

For much of this time, she was on 'country work', making chains for agricultural purposes. There was a real variety in this work, with small chains for calves contrasting with the heavy and long chains for bulls. Lucy also fashioned traces for ploughs and carts made plain, twisted or dented according to the preference of the customer. During her working life at Harry Stevens, Lucy was featured in 1950 in the *Express and Star* making cattle chains for export to Canada and America, under the heading 'Earner of Dollars'. She even made chains for lion traps.

Working so hard, there was little time for play, although there was the occasional works outing, whilst the local carnivals brought colour and excitement to the streets of the towns and villages of the Black Country. The only holiday Lucy had was when she was about 24. Mind you, that was no holiday because as it was she went hop picking for two weeks in Worcestershire, paying for her board and keep in a house through working in the fields each day.

In the late 1920s, Lucy met her chap, Jack Woodall. They did their courting walking round and round the parks. Jack was a miner at No. 3 Pit in Netherton.

There was no honeymoon, for after their wedding night they both went back to work. Two years later, Lucy had her son, Trevor, and then disaster overcame the young family. On 26 January 1932, Jack died of pneumonia. Lucy never married again. Loyalty was something ingrained in her. She had one chap and that was Jack. Having left the chain shop to rear Trevor, Lucy went back to Harry Stevens's. It was a hard bed she lay on for Lucy became the breadwinner not only for herself but also for others in her family: "I'd always got so much to do because my sister was here and her was crippled up badly with arthritis. After my sister died it left me with her Beryl (her niece), her Dad and my Mother, besides Trevor to look after".

Lucy at work at her hearth at Woodhouse's. I thank Trevor Woodall for sending me these photos and for letting me look at the many newspaper cuttings about his Mom. There is a fascinating book on Lucy's life by Rob Woolley called Midland Tales 3. Gi it sum 'ommer (1979) and an evocative short video on her called 'Lucy Woodall' by Tom Farmer and Peter Barsley (1971). These have provided much important material in the research of this article.

In 1957, Harry Stevens was bought by Samuel Woodhouse. By now there were few hand-made chainmakers left, but Lucy averred that hand-made chain was better than that which was machined and she stuck to her craft – as did Mrs Elizabeth Thompson who worked with Lucy. In January 1961, Sheila Riley of the *Express and Star* visited Woodhouse's small workshop in Cradley Heath. She was in awe of what she saw:

They work at stone work benches, each in front of a glowing red-hot furnace. The small rods of metal are pushed into the hot coke and heated until they are glowing. Then they are beaten with a hammer on the workbench into the right shape, threaded on the previous link and beaten closed.

Sparks are flying everywhere. Hot chains lie on the floors. The clang of the hammers, the roar, the sparks and the ever present danger that a careless blow could cause a lot of damage, don't make this workshop one of the most pleasant working places.

But Mrs Woodall and her colleagues love the work. They have done it all their lives like their mother and fathers before them.

Burns and bruises had seared Lucy's skin and broken her nails hundreds of times over, for she wore no protecting gloves. As for her work clothes of a blouse and old skirt and cardy covered by aprons, she made them herself with her flair for sewing, for "I wouldn't come here wearing anything that cost much money. One flash and it's full of burns."

Year after year she dedicated herself to making chain in the old way, retiring at Christmas 1969. That did not last long, for bored without her hammer in her hand she went back to work and soon after the Black Country Society showed its respect for her by making her an Honorary Vice President. At last in 1973, she packed up for good, forced into her decision by arthritis. She was 73 years old and had laboured for sixty years and a month. Despite a life of adversity and tough grind, Lucy had no regrets.

They were hard times, but they were happier, a lot happier. We was always singing, especially at night. When it was dark we'd sing the hymn tunes and during the day we'd sing the rag times. If I got my time again I'd still go on chain. I used to love it if there came an order we'd never done before. I used to think it was grand.

Although she had formally retired Lucy carried on with her podger, making peg rugs, and with raising money for good causes. Lucy Woodall knew only one way – hard work. And work hard she did. The Black Country should be proud of her and her kind. Little money did they gain for their endeavours and little money did they seek. They asked not for financial rewards but for food on the table, companions to chat with and family to care for. We, their people, owe it to them to pass on to those yet to come the dignity, the fortitude and the independent spirit of the likes of Lucy Woodall.

During the lockout of 1910, the women chainmakers of Cradley and district sang an anthem to the tune of 'Men of Harlech'

Cradley Song. Rouse Ye Women

Through years of uncomplaining
Hope and strength are waning –
Your industry
A beggar's fee,
And meagre fare was gaining.
Now a Trade Board is created,
See your pain and dearth abated,
And the Sweater's wiles checkmated
Parliament's decree.

Rouse, ye women, long enduring,
Beat no iron, blow no bellows
Till ye win the fight, ensuing,
Pay that is your due

At length the light is breaking,
The sweater's throne is shaking,
Oh, do your part,
With all your heart,
A sweeter world in making!
Stand together, strong and splendid,
In your Union till you've ended
Tyranny, and with toil blended
Beauty, Joy and Art.

Rouse, ye women, long enduring,
Beat no iron, blow no bellows
Till ye win the fight, ensuing,
Pay that is your due

Chapter 9

HOW WE WERE TAUGHT TO SPAYK A PROPER LANGUAGE

When me and our kid, Darryl, were youngsters it seemed like that all of the family used to gather at Our Mom's on a Sunday afternoon. We listened raptly as the chatter turned to the goings on down 'the old end'. Lively characters of the past were mulled over, noteworthy events of days gone by were knocked about and a forceful way of life was shaken into view. And as we took in the bustling histories of our families, their neighbourhoods and thus our region, without knowing it we also drew in the way in which these tales were told – for they were recounted in the vigorous speech of the working-class folk of south Staffordshire and north west Warwickshire, a speech which pulled us unconsciously into the origins of the English language in the West Midlands.

In my mind's eye, those many Sunday afternoons are now one and as that day sped on, our Grandad Perry would urge us not to forget that we were related to the Tipton Slasher, he would go "Well, blige me" when something happened that he wasn't too keen on or which impressed him, and he would come out with pieces of

advice like, "Never shed a clout till May is out" and "Never mek fish a one an fowl on another". Towards the end of the afternoon, he would invariably look at Our Mom and beckon her over. Sadly, Our Grandad had multiple sclerosis and couldn't walk so he'd gain Our Mom's attention by saying, "Come ere ma wench." "What's that, Our Dad", Our Mom would reply. "Gie us a piece, wench, I'm clammed." And off Our Mom would go to cut Our Grandad a piece of bread and so stop him feeling hungry.

The words of the other older members of our family were as

Two women walking up Brown Street, Kates Hill, Dudley in the early 1950s.

77

important to me. Our Nan would begenst and snever, teach us how to play glarnies and jackstones, and warn us "to mind the orse road" and "mind our language". If we'd done something wrong, she'd admonish us that we'd catch out, and if we were playing up she'd bring us to halt by belting out, "Pack it up or yoh wun arf cop it!" When we stopped at her house her'd mek us doorstep sarnies with a Cottage Loaf, pork luncheon meat and HP brown sauce, and matter-of-factly she'd point out that her leg was a-wailing her when it was giving her some jip. When me and Our Kid went to a disco, she'd ask us if we was a-wenching it and our female cousins would be cautioned about chapping it. If she daynt like someone, Our Nan couldn't abear them – and she certainly couldn't abide anyone who was a cadger and daynt pay their way or someone who never knew the meaning of work.

All the while, our Aunt Win would let us know how that her'd traipsed all over the town and that her'd had a good mooch with her ta-ta bag, the big shopping bag her took with her everywhere. If anyone was slagging someone off, Our Winnie would gently point out that "We're all God's children", but she had no time for scratters, people who were mean. Then she and Our Nan would bring to mind their mom, Great Granny Wood, the woman who hatched and dispatched in their street because she brought the babbies into the world and laid out folk when they left this world. She was a hard-collaring woman who had to mek do and mend every day of her life and could put together a filling meal with a few bacon bones and pot vegetables. Much that she bought was on the slate at the

A bustling Owen Street, Tipton in the early twentieth century.

huckster's shop, and often all she had to eat was a dish of sop – stale bread mashed up with the leavings of the tea pot. Nobody gid her nothing and day after day, her would be in the brewus, maiding and dollying, blueing and rinsing and meking sure that her own kids wore clothes that were as spotless as were those she cleaned for the better off.

With sayings and words bouncing hither and thither, Our Mom would tell us to have no cotter with someone who was upsetting us and to tek no notice if we were teased by a cousin; she'd let us know how someone had come a right purler and scraged their legs; and she'd admonish us not to let anyone see us blartin if we'd had a bit of dust up over the rec. If we were snivelling and grizzling, her'd demand that we'd pack it up and when we were really chuffed with ourselves her'd observe that "Yer in yer oiltot". If we left some food we were lectured for having eyes bigger than our bellies, and woe betide someone who didn't do what they had said they would, because they were damned as fanaging. And if we were mithering her, we'd be ordered to stop pithering about and do summat useful.

Often Our Nan's brothers, our Uncle George and our Uncle Bill would pop in and put in their tuppence worth. Our Georgie was nicknamed the fat un and he'd bring to the fore how our Great Grandad Wood, the old mon, would tek no nonsense from no-one and would have a set to with anyone, no matter how hard they were. Our Uncle Bill was the big un, the oldest lad, and once when he saw someone he daynt like he asked the person whether or not they'd got their rings on their fingers from down the suff – the drain – "where yo' come from yerself".

Our Dad worn't left out. He would fetch us over to "Goo and chuck that rubbish in the miskins", the dustbins, and when it was bedtime he'd alert us to the fact that it was time to get up the dancers, the stairs. He was always careful not to buy a pig in a poke and to save a bit and spend a bit – mind you he'd often shout out to us to draw the curtains and "Dowt the light else the bobowlers'll come in". On other occasions, when we left the door open he'd ask us if we was born in a barn and he'd order us to "Put the wood in the ole!" And if we did something foolish, he'd look at us with a withering glance and ask "Int yer gorrany oil in yer lamp, son?"

Other times, the old pot and pan would evoke a lost world of illegal betting. It was a world peopled with tekers and runners, the folk who took cash bets for illegal bookies, coppers whom you bunged to let you know when they were going to nick you, cute punters who were clever with their betting, and old dears who had a flutter for a bit of fun and who boasted colourful monikers and nom de plumes.

The old mon's uncles wornt with us on those Sundays, but their words and pronunciations were as important to me for my understanding of who we were. Born in the 1890s, neither Uncle Bill nor his younger brother, Uncle Wal, said floor or door – always they came out as flo-er and do-er, whilst cloth became clorth and hospital was orspital. To have something on credit was to have it on the mace, and somebody who was seen as a bad un was a mongrel. Putting summat in the pawnshop was popping it at Uncle's and they never tired of letting me know the number of times when they were kids that their old mon and the old lady had done a moonlight flit when they couldn't pay the rent.

Their mom, Great Granny Chinn, was a wardrobe dealer – a posh way of saying she was someone who flogged second-hand clothes – and a couple of times a wick she would tek her clobber up the old Rag Alley in Brum, lay it out on the floer and pull the buyers in with her banter. Uncle Wal mimed for me how she would lift up a pair of the old-fashioned ladies' bloomers – the type which had no covering at the

As the fog clears on a typically cold and damp November morning during the early 1950s, the weather more than likely is among the topics of conversation as two men pass the time of day on the corner of a Tipton Street.

front and were just two holes for the legs and were tied together by string. Our Great Gran would lift up the underclothes and bawl out to a woman, "Ee are ma wench. Look a' these! Ow about these! Come on now, if yo fancy a pair of freetraders these'll do y'. Come on now!"

In those days of the 1960s you didn't hear anyone talking like my family or their friends on the wireless or on the television – except for those who mocked or demeaned our accent and speech. Anyone who was well educated and in positions of authority spoke 'posh', and it is not surprising, then, that many working-class parents wanted their children to converse in Standard English. It was felt, probably rightly, that this speech would allow youngsters to get on better in life. I can understand why so many moms and dads sought for their children 'to speak properly', as they thought. It is not their fault that society was so prejudiced against dialect speakers and that those with strong accents were so often discriminated against. And I blame no mother or father who seeks to impress upon

Of course, the centre-point of many a community, the pub. This one, the 'Brown Lion' in Birmingham Street, Oldbury, was a thriving licensed premises back in 1893. The tall girl on the left is Kate Lee, then aged 16, whose granddaughter, Cynthia Baker of Oldbury, supplied this picture to the Express and Star.

their youngsters the need to speak Standard English. Indeed it is essential that everyone has a sound command of this dialect. However, it must be borne in mind that Standard English is just that – a dialect and as well as acknowledging its importance we ought also to assert the significance of local dialects.

From an early age I rebelled against the belief that the way my family spoke was wrong. In my youthful eyes, they were the ones who spoke properly. I was too young to rationalise my actions or to justify what I was doing, all I knew was that I didn't want to be different, that I wanted to speak like Our Nan and Grandad, Our Winnie and Our Georgie, my Uncle Bill and my Uncle Wal. They are all dead now, but I know that they were proud not only that one of them got on academically, but also that I continued to be one of them and did not forsake their tongue.

Now that I am older, I can express my feelings about my language. I have benefited from a good education, an education that was denied to all the members of my family until I came along. I have had a choice to do with my life what I wish, a gift that was withheld from all my forebears until my time. I can be who I want to be and speak as I wish to. And still I wish to speak like them. For they made me that which I am. They scratted and collared, toiled and moiled so that someone in the future had a future, had opportunities, had possibilities. I owe it to them to grasp hold of the chances that they laboured for but also I owe a duty to them not to turn my back on their lives. I shall never forget that debt nor that responsibility and so never will I seek to pretend that I do not come from them. I will speak as they did for if I forswear their dialect I will have cast aside my heritage and disowned my family.

God knows that our folk had nothing to give us in terms of money and property. They had no gold nor silver, nor houses or lands, nor jewellery or finery. Yet, they passed on to us precious things. They gave us their examples of hard work. They showed us how to make strong neighbourhoods in the midst of a dark and hostile environment. And they handed us their words. Even if they are no longer used commonly, we have a responsibility to give our words to our children and to their children. For these words make us hark back to the beginnings of our region and to those who made us first. If we abandon our words as worthless we give up our past as meaningless. And if we do that we throw out something vital of ourselves, for a people who lose their language are a people who lose their soul.

These are things I feel deep in my heart and my being. They are made all the more powerful by the years of my research in which tens of thousands of Black Country folk and Brummies have shared their lives with me. And now I understand fully that our speech is not slang and should not be denigrated. It has a long and distinguished history.

Some Black Country Sayings

Allus in the lezzer when yoh orter be in the lairne – in the wrong place at the wrong time.

As big as a bonk oss – as big as one of the large horses that worked on the pit bonks.

Doh tek a blind bit a notice – ignore something or someone's actions or comments.

E con dish it out but he cor tek it – someone who is quick to criticise but slow to take criticism.

E day know A (or B) from a bull's foot – someone who was ignorant.

Er's got a voice on her like a glede under a dooer – a harsh, scraping sound, like an ember from the fire scraping under the door.

Give a mon a bairsin o broth an it im over the yed with the spewn – to give with one hand and take with another.

Gooin all round the Wrekin – going the long way round to get somewhere, or someone who is long winded in speech.

Got ossmuck in is shoes – to someone who has grown quickly.

Is faerther woe be jed so long as e's alive – to someone who is the spitting image of his dad.

Like aving an opple when yowve got false teeth – having something that's no good to you.

Marry the miskin (ash heap or midden) for the muck and get pizened with the poison on it – marry for money and be embittered by it.

May the Devil run through thee booted and spurred with a scythe on its back – a curse known as the Sedgley Curse.

Nicky Nicky Note

Shoe the lickle cote (colt)

Ere a nail and theer a nail

And tek fast ote.

A nursery rhyme for babies like 'This Little Piggy'.

Shift yer feet from up the ess hole – stop lounging around and do something. The Ess hole was the ash hole in the fire.

The blartin (crying) cow soon forgets its calf – a bereaved person who makes a show of his or her grief at a death.

Thee cosn cuss like thee cudst, cost? – You cannot curse like you could curse, can you?

There ay no babby washed – nothing's been done.

Traipsin in an out like a dog at a fair – going around aimlessly.

To eat like a pig chibbling coal – to eat noisily.

To fly off the ondle – to get really angry.

To put the beans to bile (boil) – to put up the marriage banns.

To rattle like a bibble in a can – to chatter incessantly.

Chapter 10

IT BAIN'T BAD ENGLISH
JUST AN ECHO OF THE PAST

"Ow bist?" – a more fascinating way to ask "How are you?", this phrase may not be spoken as commonly as once it was, but still it can be heard, especially amongst older men, as a form of greeting around the Rowley Hills. So can its reply, "I baint too bad". Both are powerful expressions, harking back as they do to the origins of the English people and the beginnings of the English language. For the word bist is the German for "are", whilst baint is not bad grammar as some would claim wrongly, instead it comes from "be not" and as such is the negated form of the first person singular of the verb "to be". Such phrases have been spoken for almost fifteen hundred years in the Black Country and they call out to us that Black Country speech should not be demeaned and denigrated rather that it should be cherished and honoured and, most importantly, kept alive.

There are many other words spoken between Wedgfield and Bramich, Darlo and Quarry Bonk that connect us indelibly with our forebears. When a babby is blartin we are speaking in the manner of the Anglo Saxons who settled hereabouts from the mid 500s onwards. For babby is from babban, meaning baby, whilst blartin derives from blaetan, signifying the bleating of sheep – and the noise made by a sheep can be compared to that of crying. Those Anglo-Saxon settlers would also have appreciated our use of wench. Coming from wencel, a child, it changed slightly to become a young maid. Today, when we speak of wenches we still mean young women, except in the case of Our Wench, who is a big sister who minded her siblings and acted as a little mother – and in the process gave up her own childhood and teenage years for the good of the family. We should not abandon such a word because outsiders incorrectly and ignorantly view it as degrading.

Similarly, when we chuck something in the miskins, the dustbins, we are using a term that signified dung to the Anglo Saxons and which then began to mean dung heap. Of course, each village had such a midden and, during the Industrial Revolution, when the country folk poured into Dudley and Tipton, Wednesbury and Bilston and elsewhere looking for work they brought this word with them. At first in the urban setting, the miskins was the area in a yard where the rubbish was thrown and later the name was adapted to the dustbins themselves when such a facility was introduced.

If we demand of someone to "Get that down yer wassin!", their throat, we are clinging fast to the Old English word wasend, indicating gullet; if we talk of housen and not houses we are rightly adopting the old Anglo-Saxon plural of "an" and "en" rather than the more modern "es"; and if we pronounce that we can't abear someone because we don't like them or can't endure them, then we are talking as did our ancestors who employed the word aboeran – and as did the great Elizabethan poet, Edmund Spenser. In his most famous work, "The Faerie Queene" (1590-6) he wrote in Book V, "So did the faerie knight himself abeare, And stouped oft his head from shame to shield."

Similarly if we refer to glowing embers or red-hot cinders from a fire as gledes then we bond ourselves with one of the greatest ever writers in the English language – William Chaucer. For in "The Reeve's Tale" he penned the lines, "Four gleedes have we, which I shall devyse." Regarded by many as the writer who beckoned Middle English into Modern English, Chaucer was not alone in using words with which we would be familiar in his plays. So too did Shakespeare. In the "Winter's Tale", Act IV, Scene IV, he writes "Clam your tongues and not a word more" – indicating clearly the

An Arthur Arrowsmith line drawing of Lower Green, Tettenhall – from a few years ago – where it is said, Edward the Elder defeated the Danes in the year 910 – although it may have taken place in Wednesfield.

need to starve the tongues of words. We know immediately what he means for in the Black Country clammed means hungry. In speaking such an expressive word we are recalling the German word klemmen, which means to pinch – and we can easily see the tie-in because of the phrase to be pinched with hunger.

So why is it that crucial words in Black Country dialect should connect us with Germany? Well, the history of people in the West Midlands stretches back deep into the millennia BC. There have been finds of Old Stone Age tools, left behind by hunters passing through the region and there is evidence from the Sandwell Valley to indicate the presence of hunter-gatherers from the Middle Stone Age. Later, during the Iron Age, it would seem that settlement in the West Midlands was marginal and that the region fell across the borders of two Celtic tribes: the Cornovii to the north west and the Corieltauvi to the north east. These peoples were overcome by the Romans in the first century AD, and once they had been pacified each boasted a capital – Wroxeter and Leicester respectively. There is no evidence of anything so substantial in our area, although the Romans did establish a fort at Metchley in the modern Edgbaston.

But if human activity locally can be traced back thousands of years, then it was the Germanic invaders of the West Midlands who have left their mark most firmly upon our area, both in our place names and language. Arriving from the mid-400s

A steam tram passes over the bridge of the River Tame at the foot of Holloway Bank, Hill Top in 1898. The Tame forms the valley in which the towns and villages of the north Black Country developed.

from what is now northern Germany and southernmost Denmark, large numbers of Angles, Saxons and Jutes settled heavily on the coastal lands of the east and south of what was to become England. In particular, so great were the numbers of migrating Angles that Bede, in his "History of the English Church and People" (written in the early eighth century), declared that their land of Angulus "is said to remain unpopulated to this day".

Not much is known about the emergence of the Angles in the English Midlands but it seems that they made an invasion in the early 500s from the stronghold of East Anglia. It is likely that the move into the Midlands came along rivers like the Trent and its tributaries such as the Tame, which forms the valley into which fall the towns and villages of the north Black Country; and it also appears that these pioneers did not take over from the Welsh in a sudden conquest. Instead they came as groups of men and women under the command of a leader seeking land. Consequently, many of the Welsh were neither exterminated nor beaten out and it may be that both peoples co-existed and inter-married with each other.

A few place names recall the Welsh who once controlled this land. Penkridge in Staffordshire relates to Pennocrucio, the Latin form of the Romano-British Pennocrucium, a Roman station two miles south of the modern village. The Roman name itself is made up of the Old Welsh words penn, meaning hill or headland, and crug, signifying a burial mound – traces of which are near to Rowley Hill Farm. Upper Penn and Lower Penn share the same derivation from this ancient word for hill, whilst Barr in Barr Beacon and Great Barr also means hill top in Old Welsh. By contrast, Lichfield means the open land, from the Anglo-Saxon word feld, at or close to Lyccid, the grey wood. Thos pre-Welsh name led to Letocetum, the Roman name for Wall. Then there is Walsall, which may mean the halh, the nook or valley of land, of the Welsh; and the River Tame, perhaps indicating dark one or flow in Old Welsh, and itself arising from a pre-Celtic word.

Amongst the Angles who came to make their home in the West Midlands was a leader called Beorma whose ingas, people, joined him in setting up a ham, a landed estate or homestead which became known as Birmingham. It may well be that Beorma and his followers took control of an area larger than that of the old manor of Birmingham. Whatever the case, Beorma's folk would have arrived by the late 500s, at a time when there was no great kingdom in the region and when the political situation was in a state of flux. Another such tribal leader may have been Esne. He and his ingas, the Esningas, set up or took over from the Welsh, a tun, a farmstead or manor which was recorded in a document from 996 as Esingetun and which has now changed but slightly to become Essington. Other folk groups included the Husmerae, in and around what we know as Kidderminster and brought to mind now by the district of Ismere; the Pencesaete of the Penkridge area; and the Tomsaete along the Tame and in the locality of Tamworth and Lichfield.

From the early 600s the Essingas, Beormingas and other tribal groups were brought under the sway of the Mierce, the boundary people. They probably took their name from the fact that they were the marcher people with the Welsh. Their heartland was around Lichfield and Tamworth in Staffordshire and under a ruler called Penda, who was in power till 655, a powerful kingdom called Mercia was forged. This fierce king is brought to mind today in Penda's ford, that is Upper Pendeford Farm and Lower Pendeford Farm, close to Codsall. An even earlier Mercian king, Pybba, is kept alive in Pedmore, Stourbridge – this name meaning Pybba's moor or marsh.

The whole of the Black Country and most of Birmingham would have been part of Mercia. North Worcestershire and the rest of Warwickshire would have come under another kingdom, that of Hwicce, which also became part of Mercia.

Under first King Aethelbald (716-57) and then King Offa (757-96), Mercia became the most powerful kingdom in Anglo-Saxon England. By this time, the descendants of the original Welsh inhabitants of Mercia were increasingly mixed with the Anglo-Saxons – so much so that there was little difference between the two peoples away from border areas in Herefordshire and Shropshire – and by the later 800s, the speaking of Welsh had disappeared from most of the West Midlands. This was the case especially in north Warwickshire, Staffordshire and north-east Worcestershire.

Market Street, Penkridge during heavy rains in 1958, with residents lending a hand to move a stranded car. The name of the village refers to Pennocrucium, a Roman station two miles south of the modern village.

Following the death of Offa, Mercia continued to impose itself as a major force, but by the 820s Wessex – the kingdom of the West Saxons – had taken over as the most important Anglo-Saxon kingdom. Within a generation, however, all of Anglo-Saxon England was assailed by raiders from Scandinavia, and from the 850s, Danish forces began to stay throughout the year and not return home in the winter. Beset by rivalry between two dynasties claiming the kingship, Mercia was wracked by internal divisions and further weakened by short-term rulers. Still, it was a large and potentially strong kingdom and did not fall beneath the Vikings as East Anglia and the once powerful Northumbria. Then in 874 the great Viking army marched unopposed into the heart of Mercia. In the wake of this humiliation, King Burgred was deposed and driven into exile. He was replaced by Ceolwulf II from the opposing dynasty, a leader

Resident Arthur Cope outside the 'Old Mitre' pub in Essington in the early 1900s. The village name derives from an Anglo-Saxon leader called Esne.

who had to acknowledge Viking overlordship. By 877, Mercia was partitioned between an eastern section under the thrall of the Vikings and a western and southern portion that remained under Anglo-Saxon control.

Free Mercia was to play a vital role in the making of England. That it did so was due in great measure to a Mercian earldorman called Aethelred. His power base was around Gloucester and it was he who forged a potent and successful alliance with Alfred the Great of Wessex. Within a few years of the splitting of his kingdom, Ceolwulf II disappeared from history and it seems that Lord Aethelred began to gain the support of other Mercian earls. Although acting as a king he never assumed a royal title, even after he married Alfred's daughter, Lady Aethelflaed, herself descended from Mercian royalty on her mother's side. With their reorganised armies and newly-built burhs, fortified settlements, Alfred and Aethelred were formidable opponents. No longer on the back foot, the forces of Mercia and Wessex

– singly and jointly – took the attack to the Vikings.

Aethelred won famous victories, perhaps the most momentous of all at the Battle of Tettenhall in 910. The year before, Aethelred and Edward the Elder, Alfred's son and successor, had led a sustained raid on territory belonging to the Danes of Northumbria. Enraged, these Vikings invaded Mercia. Reaching the River Avon they struck north and crossed the Severn. After despoiling the land and taking much plunder, they began the return to their kingdom. After crossing the Severn at Bridgnorth they were surprised by a large army of Anglo-Saxons on the site of the Lower Green at Tettenhall, although some sources indicate the battle was at Wednesfield. They met on 5 August and according to "The Anglo-Saxon Chronicle", the army of the West Saxons and the Mercians came upon their enemies from behind "when it was on its way home, and fought with them. They put the force to flight and killed many of them".

Lichfield market stall holder, Beatrice James, pictured with a customer in 1970. Lichfield takes its name from both Anglo-Saxon and British (Welsh) place names.

Later that year, Aetheled's wife, Aethelflaed seems to have taken control of West Mercia because of the illness or wounding of her husband who died soon after in 911. She is the only woman who ruled an Anglo-Saxon kingdom. That she was able to do so was due not only to her blood but also to her redoubtable character. Tough, motivated and inspirational she must have been. Aethelflaed continued the policy of making fortified settlements, such as those at Tamworth and Stafford in 913 and at Warwick in 914. Not a woman to sit at home whilst her men fought, she also led her forces into battle and in 917 she took the offensive against the Danes. The Anglo-Saxon Chronicle notes that "this year Ethelfleda, lady of the Mercians, with the help of God. before Laminas, conquered the town called Derby, with all that thereto belonged; and there were also slain four of her thanes, that were most dear to her, within the gates". Aware of her victory, a year later the Vikings of Leicester surrendered to her, whilst the Danes of York promised to submit to her. They were unable to fulfil their pledges because Aethelflaed died on 12 June at Tamworth.

Remembered today by a statue in Tamworth, Aethelflaed, the Lady of the Mercians, was also responsible for the upbringing of a man who became the first king of England. Athelstan was he. The grandson of Alfred the Great and son of Edward the Elder, Athelstan was the greatest ruler in these islands since the Roman forces had pulled out five hundred years before. Acclaimed as the emperor of the whole world of Britain, he was raised amongst the people of West Mercia and spoke with our dialect. His name meant noble stone, and Athelstan lived up to that high name. When his father died in 924, the West Mercians supported him as ruler and the people of Wessex soon followed in acclaiming him as king. In the next few years, Athelstan conquered the Danish kingdom of York – now ruled by Norsemen from Dublin – and brought in what was left of English Northumbria. The most powerful ruler in Britain, Athelstan was feared and in 937 his enemies came together in a great force of Scots, Britons from Strathclyde and Norse from Dublin. They were shattered by the Anglo-Saxons at Brunanburgh. Athelstan's feat was acclaimed in a poem.

Here
Athelstan king,
of earls the lord,
rewarder of heroes,
and his brother eke (also)
Edmund atheling,
elder of ancient race,
slew in the fight,
with the edge of their swords,
the foe at Brunanburgh!
The sons of Edward
their board-walls clove,
and hewed their banners,
with the wrecks of their hammers.
So were they taught
by kindred zeal,
that they at camp oft
'gainst any robber
their land should defend,
their hoards and homes.
Pursuing fell

the Scottish clans;
the men of the fleet
in numbers fell;
'midst the din of the field
the warrior swate.
Since the sun was up
in morning-tide,
gigantic light!
glad over grounds,
God's candle bright,
eternal Lord! —
'till the noble creature
sat in the western main:
there lay many
of the Northern heroes
under a shower of arrows,
shot over shields;
and Scotland's boast,
a Scythian race,
the mighty seed of Mars!
With chosen troops,
throughout the day,
the West-Saxons fierce
press'd on the loathed bands;
hew'd down the fugitives,
and scatter'd the rear,
with strong mill-sharpen'd blades,
The Mercians too
the hard hand-play
spared not to any
of those that with Anlaf
over the briny deep
in the ship's bosom
sought this land
for the hardy fight.

In a violent age, Athelstan was a mighty leader but he was also regarded as a just, learned and generous ruler – especially towards the common people. Writing in the twelfth century and taking his evidence from an older work, William of Malmesbury declared that:

He was easy and charming with the servants of God, affable and courteous to the laymen, serious out of regard for his majesty to the magnates; friendly and down to earth with the lesser folk, out of sympathy for their poverty, putting aside the pride of kingship. He was as we have learnt not beyond what is becoming in stature, and slender in body; his hair as we have ourselves seen from his relics, flaxen, beautifully plaited with braids of gold. He was much beloved by his subjects out of admiration of his courage and humility, but like a thunderbolt to rebels by his invincible steadfastness.

Athelstan died in 939 in his middle age. A West Saxon by birth and descent, a West Mercian by upbringing and speech he forged England from upon the anvil of the Dark Ages. He could not have done so without the people of Staffordshire, Worcestershire and Warwickshire.

Chapter 11

REAL PLACES IN HISTORY FOR NAMES STILL IN USE

Lady Wulfrun – probably the most important person in the history of Wolverhampton. It was she, an Anglo-Saxon noblewoman, who gave her name to the modern city, which means the high estate – Heantune – of Wulfrun. Her statue stands close to the historic parish church of Saint Peter and it is after her that the people of Wolverhampton are called Wulfrunians. But who was this woman? Certainly, she was a person of some standing and was recognised as such by her contemporaries. She first comes to notice in 943, just four years after the death of Athelstan – the first king of England and the man who had led his Mercian and West Saxon fighters in crushing his Welsh, Danish and Scots enemies at the Battle of Brunaburh.

But with the death of the mighty Athelstan, the Vikings regained their vigour and England was wracked by war. Led by the Norse king of Dublin, Olaf Guthfrithson, the Viking forces rampaged across the land and split apart the kingdom of England. Lady Wulfrun was one of the victims of the fierce conflict. In 943, Olaf stormed the old Mercian capital of Tamworth and as the Worcester Chronicle recorded, "there was great slaughter on both sides; the Danes had the victory and carried away great booty with them. On this raid Wulfrun was taken prisoner." Wulfrun was important enough to be mentioned by name and as a person of consequence it is likely that she was held for ransom by the Viking leaders.

Later freed from her captors, she is noted again in 985, at a time when Danish raiders were again ravaging and pillaging. In that year, Aethelred, damned as The Unready, granted ten portions of land at Heantune and one at Treselcotum to Wulfrun in perpetuity. The bounds of her lands as given in this grant survived as parish boundaries of Wolverhampton for over 800 years. They included the Goose Brook, a tributary of the Smestow Brook, and recalled in Gorsebrook Road. Here is to be found "Wulfruna's Well", a memorial on the supposed site of an ancient spring. Other boundary features were the Penn Brook and the Smestow Brook itself, given in its old Celtic name as the Tresel, perhaps meaning strongly flowing, and brought to mind today in Trysull.

Despite the Danish invasion and later the rule of Danish kings, Anglo Saxon triumphed as the language spoken across the country. That is not to say that Norse did not have an impact. It did and many modern English words are from the Norse – such as fellow, score and beck. These and other words came to be part of the English language, and it is evident that in the formerly Danish-controlled parts of England that Norse had an even more pervasive influence on the local dialect. However, in West Mercia, which included the modern Black Country, the linguistic effect of the Danes was restricted to those words that entered general usage. Similarly, Norse place names are largely absent west and south of the Watling Street, the dividing line between English and Danish Mercia.

Thus in the Black Country the overwhelming majority of the place names are Anglo Saxon. Bilston is mentioned in Lady Wulfrun's charter, and a few years later in 996 was given as Bilsetnatun, meaning the farmstead – tun – of the dwellers on the sharp ridge – bill saete. Nearby, Tipton was first recorded as Tibintone and means the estate – tun – called after a certain Tibba. Sedgley, too, is noted in the charter as Segleslei, signifying the woodland clearing or glade – ley – of man called Secg. Similarly, Dudley is the clearing of a chap named Dudda, whilst Rowley is the rough – ruh – woo or clearing. To the north, Willenhall is one of the earliest Black Country place names cited in a document. In 732 it was given as Willenhalch and as such was the nook or valley –halh – of Willa.

Wednesfield may be as old. It harks back to the period when the Anglo-Saxons believed in the old gods and had not become Christians, for it is the open land – feld – of Woden. Although it is first noted in 996 as Wodensfeld, the name suggest a much earlier origin for the people of our region would have become Christians by the late seventh century. Woden himself was the greatest of the old gods, the creator, the god of victory and of the dead. He is remembered in Wednesday – Woden's day – and also in Wednesbury. The stronghold – burgh – of Woden, it is not mentioned in documents until the Domesday Book of 1066 but again, its name indicates a much older origin. By contrast Oldbury does not gain written attention until

A girl with her ball in Owen Street, Tipton in the middle years of the twentieth century. Tipton was first recorded as Tibintone in the Domesday Book of 1086.

1174, but it too signifies a fortification – in its case, an old one. Interestingly, many older people still refer to West Bromwich as Bromwich or Bramwich and the place was first given as just Bromwic in 1086. It is not recorded as Westbromwich until 1322, by which time it was the west dwelling or farm – wich – where grew the broom – brom.

The statue of Lady Wulfrun outside Saint Peter's, Wolverhampton. Lady Wulfrun gave her name to Wolverhampton and its people are called Wulfrunians after her.

How then did the Anglo-Saxons of our region speak? Like all their folk from Northumbria in the north to Sussex in the south and from Essex in the east to Wessex in the west, their language was Old English. This was a Germanic speech which emerged amongst the Angles, Saxons, Jutes, Frisians and other groups from northern Germany and Denmark who arrived in the former Roman province of Britannia. Apart from a few inscriptions written in the runic alphabet, little written material survives from the fifth and sixth centuries and thus most of the evidence for the Old English language dates from the time of King Alfred (849-99).

By this period, Old English had emerged as a distinct form of speech with various dialects. Because of the success of its kings like Alfred and their role in the making of the kingdom of England, the particular form of Old English belonging to Wessex became the dominant form for writing for most Old English texts. This dialect was spoken south of the Thames, except in Kent. It is relevant to point out, however, that many later West Saxon texts do indicate a Mercian influence. This was because Mercian scholars were brought in by Alfred to help the literary rebirth which he energised. Elsewhere in England, Northumbrian held sway above the line made by the Mersey and Humber Rivers, thus embracing most of northern England and the eastern lowlands of Scotland. Finally, Mercian

Saint Peter's Church at the turn of the twentieth century.

was the dialect of the folk of the Midlands, East Anglia and also the London districts – for this had belonged to Mercia.

Like Northumbria, Mercia was a great area and it is not known if before the Danish conquests there were distinctions in the speech between its eastern and western localities, or indeed between its northern and southern districts. Unfortunately, there survive very few texts written in the Mercian dialect. However, those that do remain indicate that the Mercians turned an "a" into an "o" before a nasal consonant such as "n", "m" and "ng". Thus Mercians would have said mon for man, hond for hand and lond for land. It is remarkable that this feature survived strongly into the twentieth century in the Black Country and Birmingham. This distinctive pronunciation remains strong today as in "Gie it some ommer!", the phrase urging someone to give it some hammer, hit something with strength; and in our familiar word for mother – mom. It is sad that officialdom decrees that at school

Children play in Wilkes Street, Willenhall in April 1965. Willenhall is one of the earliest recorded Black Country place names and was Willanhalch in a document dated 733. It means the nook or valley – halh – of man called Willa.

our children should be taught that the correct term is mum. It is not correct in the West Midlands. I look forward to the day when our youngsters are able to use the word mom without having the "o" crossed out and replaced by a "u" and when we will be able to buy cards dedicated to Mom on Mother's Day.

Following the Norman Conquest, the English became a subject people. Anglo Saxon now was the speech of the conquered and the dispossessed for French was the language of government, administration, literature and the Church – although Latin was used also in religious and administrative affairs. But the English tongue was not overwhelmed as had been the speech of the Celts when the Angles and Saxons had taken over what became England. Spoken by the great majority of the population, Anglo Saxon proved itself to be hardy and adaptable and by the later twelfth century it had evolved into Middle English – a form which is more recognisable to speakers of Modern English.

Flourishing among the common people, and now the first language of the nobility, Middle English burst fully upon the national scene in the fourteenth century with a wonderful array of literature. Crucially, each work was put down in the dialect of the speaker, for there was no such thing as Standard English. By this time, scholars have identified a number of major dialects: Northern, which covered the same area as the Old English kingdom of Northumbria; Southern, equating to the former kingdom of Wessex; Kentish in Kent; East Midland, holding sway over East Anglia and the eastern midlands; and West Midland or West Central, which was dominant in south Lancashire, Cheshire, Shropshire, Herefordshire, Warwickshire, Worcestershire and Staffordshire – equating mostly to that part of Mercia which had not been conquered by the Danes.

Some dialect experts further sub-divide this area and recognise a Staffordshire dialect which embraces Staffordshire itself, most of Cheshire, northern Shropshire, parts of southern Derbyshire, north-western Warwickshire and north-eastern Worcestershire. Whatever the fine distinctions, it must be borne in mind that dialects cannot be demarcated easily. They merge one into the other and the borders of a certain feature of speech may not fall on the line drawn by referring to another peculiarity. Still, it is obvious that what is now the Black Country and Birmingham fell clearly within the bounds of the West Midlands dialect, a distinct form of Middle English which had emerged from Anglo Saxon and was less affected by Norse influences.

William Chaucer, the famed writer of "The Canterbury Tales", recognised the varieties of English when he bemoaned the "gret diversité / In Englissh and in wryting of oure tonge", (Troilus, 5. 1793-4). Compared to the Anglo-Saxon period, when most texts were written in the dialect of Wessex, and the Modern English period when a Standard English form of writing emerged, there is no recognised speech for the writing of Middle English. Instead, as Chaucer indicated, poets and others all wrote in their regional tongue. Several major Middle English texts have been brought to us by people who lived in the West Midlands. Amongst them were Layamon's Brut, written about 1200. This poem tells the history of Britain and was written by a man who was the parish priest of Areley Kings in Worcestershire.

Another important poem is" Sir Gawain and the Green Knight", written in the dialect of the north-west Midlands by someone who may have come from the borders of Cheshire and Staffordshire. Thus the author would have fallen within the general area of the West Mercian variation of Middle English. He was also responsible for the poems "Pearl", "Cleanness (or Purity)" and "Patience" – all dating from the later 1300s. "Sir Gawain" is an epic Arthurian poem and at its beginning a gigantic green stranger at King Arthur's court challenges any man to strike him with an waxe "so long as I shall have leave to launch a return blow Barlay". Here barlay means free and unchecked and it is not hard to see how the word came to be used by kids in the Black

A view of Bilston town centre, featuring a Carver's lorry, from the late 1960s. The name comes from Bilsetnatun, meaning the settlement – tun – of the dwellers – saeten – on the sharp ridge – bill. It is mentioned in a charter from 985.

Country and Birmingham in their play and when they wanted a break, as in a game a of tig or whatever when a break is wanted and a child calls out "Barley" or "!Arley barley!". The author also uses her instead of she as many of us still would in phrases like "Who does er think er is?" or "Er dunarf fancy erself er does!" Her in this sense is from the Anglo Saxon word heo meaning she.

There are a number of other texts from our dialect region such as "Ancrene Wise", and "St Erkenwald". This last includes the use of the word brevit for reported. Coming from the Anglo Saxon word gebrefan it came to mean rummaging around, as in "I've been breviting and come across some good stuff". Perhaps the greatest Middle English work in our dialect is "The Vision of Piers Plowman", a radical and challenging piece that looks to the marked reform of society and asserts the belief that, following the example of Piers the Plowman, everyone should contribute to society. It was written in the later 1300s by a man who was probably brought up either in the Malvern Hills in Worcestershire or in the Clee Hills in Shropshire. In *The Vision* he makes three references to the Malvern Hills and its affinity with our speech is proclaimed by the way in which words like banke are written as bonke, the "a" becoming an "o".

Langland's work is noted as the most widely read of the Middle English alliterative poems – a form popular in the Midlands and the North. It was not the style used by his contemporary, Geoffrey Chaucer, the man who is praised as the first great poet of the English nation and who is regarded as gaining prestige for the written language of the London dialect. Neither Chaucer's work nor its profound effect on the development of the English language should be lessened, but neither should we neglect the importance of literature from the West Midlands dialect region. And we should also recognise that Chaucer himself used words that may have died out elsewhere in the country but which can still be heard in the Black Country. Words like mullock for mess or rubbish. In his "Reeves Tale", Chaucer writes "That ilke fruit is ever lenger the wers, Til it be rotten in mollock or in street".

Sedgley High Street and Bull Ring from 1910. The town's name is derived from Secgesleage, signifying the wood or woodland clearing or glade – ley – of a man called Secg.

By the later 1400s, Middle English itself had developed into Early Modern English. Great changes continued to occur in the language before Modern English fully emerged in the 1700s. And changes are taking place still. However, despite the development of a Standard English in both the spoken and written word, the basic dialect map of England remains mostly the same as it had been in the Middle English period and so do the key differences between the dialects. With the influence of television programmes and films, how much longer dialects can flourish is questionable. Still, we should not give in easily to the tide of transatlantic words and pronunciations, for if we do and allow our words to disappear then we will have wiped from our lives who we are and where we come from. We will become as nobodies with no past and no memory. Black Country speech calls out to us our identity and ties us to our forebears and our region. Speak it proudly.

Piers Plowman: The Prologue

In a somer sesun, whon softe was the sonne,
I schop (made) me into a shroud, as I a scheep were;
In habite as an hermite unholy of werkes
Wente I wyde in this world wondres to here;
Bote in a Mayes morwnynge on Malverne hulles
Me bifel a ferly (a marvel), of fairie, me-thoughte.
I was wery, forwandred (astonished), and wente me to reste
Undur a brod bonke bi a bourne side;
And as I lay and leonede and lokede on the watres,
I slumbrede in a slepynge, hit swyed so murie (joyful).
Thenne gon I meeten a mervelous sweven (sleep),
That I was in a wildernesse, wuste I never where;
And as I beheold into the est an heigh to the sonne,
I sauh a tour on a toft, tryelyche (truly) i-maket;
A deop dale bineothe, a dungun ther-inne,
With deop dich and derk and dredful of sighte.
A feir feld full of folk fond I ther bitwene,
Of alle maner of men, the mene and the riche,
Worchinge and wandringe as the world asketh.

Chapter 12

RECALLING OUR SAYINGS
FROM DAYS OF THE PAST

It's a Day Good-day

Janice Williams of **Yew Tree Lane, Tettenhall**, is originally from Blakenhall and she enjoyed the articles on Black Country dialect: "Such memories from my childhood came flooding back. Here are a few sayings I recall from those far-off days. You'll probably know most, but maybe some will be less familiar. Here goes!

Wouldn't stop a pig in an entry! – for someone who was bow-legged or bandy-legged.
Bin it on the ead with a crowbar – referring to someone with a flat hairstyle.
A streak a lightning – a tall thin person.
A pairer braces – a thin person.
Fiddle features – a thin-faced person.
A face like a full moon – a round-faced person.
Fairy footed – someone prone to trip up easily.
A fog orn – loud voiced person.
A big fat swasum – a very fat lady.
A brazen Jezebel – a loose' woman.
A pimple on a round of beef – a small hat on a large head.
A cat's chorus – a less than tuneful rendition of a song.
Passed all through – passed all the exams.
A fairy elephant – a dancer not light on his or her feet.
As ard as a bibble – food as hard to chew as a pebble.
As straight as eights – very straight hair.
A dumbcluck – someone not too clever.
Too slow to catch a cold – self explanatory!
Clodoppers – big or oversized shoes.
Es all there with is cough drops – he's very intelligent.
I've been meeting meself coming back – I've been rushed off me feet.
It's A-day-Good-day – God sends Sunday with you – You're always putting things
    off and they never get done.

My favourite Black Country phrase of all is one you must be so familiar with. To a 'foreigner' not from these parts how can 'Ah day goo' possibly mean 'I did not go'. What fun it is to conjure them all up from our childhood."

Sticking with My Dialect

Kath Butler, nee Flavell, now of **Bradley** grew up in **Dartmouth Crescent, the Lunt**. She had wonderful parents and a very loving childhood. There was no money but all five children were loved very much. Kath went to Etheridge School and "when we came home from school and had had tea, we would all congregate at the Bank (Dartmouth Crescent) and play skipping, tin-can-a-larkie, top and whip, marbles – and every other game you could mention. There were us lot (the Flavells), the Dolmans, the Webbs, the Turpins, the Howells and many more. We would go over the fields at the back of our house. Beddows Field was full of cows and we would run between them and go and jump the Rusty Brook and go over to the Open 'Oles and watch them fish and carry on over the Bridge to Darlaston Park."

Kath's dad worked on the boats on the canal for Tooly's coal yard, but finished up at the steel works in Bilston. She says "I can't talk posh. I tried and feel a fool, so I'm sticking with my own dialect and proud of it". Her Gran would say, 'Do get that suck stuck down yer wazin. I cor gerrit out' – don't get that sweet stuck down your throat." Then there are a number of sayings used by Kath's Mom and Dad:

"Do keep pullin them maygrums (keep pulling faces) you'll send the milk sour.
Shift them shommuck (heavy feet) away from the fire yowll gerra blister on yer toe – move your feet away from the fire or you'll burn your feet.
Ar do no, I cor see to feel – I can't see in the dark.
It's black over Arry's – it's going to rain.
I'm that dry I cor spit a tanner – I'm thirsty.
Goo up the wooden ills and pretty buttercup – go upstairs and bring the bucket up.
Come and get yer loffin gear round this – come and have your dinner.
Er con cry quicker than a duck can quack – she can cry over nothing.
What you mooching after? – what are you looking for?
Do keep messin with yo nose you'll have pig's food grown on the end – self explanatory.
These terters ay a bit a good they got more eyes than arry's riddle – these potatoes have a lot of black spots on them.
Ers gorra ferce like a fourpunny ock – She is not very pleased."

Ow We Spake

One day Councillor Steve Melia of **Friar Park Road, Wednesbury** was having a pint with his dad and his mate in the 'Three Horseshoes' pub on **Toll End Road Tipton**, when "my dad stood up and said that he was going 'round the back' and, as he left the table he said to us, 'now thee shert shift shast'?, meaning 'you will not go away will you". Steve remembers with dismay the way in which the speech of his people was derided. He attended Walton Road junior school in Friar Park and recalls that "I, like you, spoke exactly like my parents and siblings (but not quite as my grandparents) and whenever I used expressions such as "Yow cort" or "I ay a gooin to" within range of one particular teacher, which was often, I would get a back hander round the ears and cut glass "We do not speak like that round here". On the one occasion that I answered, "Well, we do at our house," I was walloped with the stick for being impertinent. I suffered for my language.

"In the seventies I spoke to a person at Sandwell Education. I wanted to trial run an evening class and the topic was to be our local language. I was swiftly told, in other words, that I was barmy to even think of such a retrograde step. In the mid eighties, and as the Deputy Mayor of Sandwell, I was guest of honour at a Saturday afternoon prize presentation at another local school. The awards were for youngsters attending classes to study the history and languages of their parents, which was Indian. In my short speech I told them how fortunate they were that they had the opportunity to learn about their roots. Mine had been beaten out of me."

An Arthur Arrowsmith illustration of Red Hill School in Zoar Street, Lower Gornal from the 1950s. Mr C. Smith, who wrote in to correct Carl on a saying, lives nearby.

War-time damage in Carlton Road, Blakenhall, where it is thought, the bomber was heading for Fischer Bearings – a German company before the war broke out. Janice Williams had a flood of memories when she read Carl's articles on our dialect. She hails from Blakenhall.

"Last year I was at the Aberystwyth hospital, where my brother was in recovery from chest problems and, in the next bed was a fellow who, after my brother and I had been chatting for some time, suddenly exclaimed with a decided Welsh lilt, 'You Black Country folk don-arf talk funny. When I was the manager of the slate quarry we used to have your boys come up to work for us and one morning one of them came into the office and asked if we had any plonks,' (me and my brother burst out laughing). 'It took ages before we found out that he was looking for planks.' That did it. I sent him one of my booklets I have been working on, on and off, for some years. I give them away to anyone who I think might be interested in the area." Steve has kindly sent me one of those booklets. It is called *A Black Country Dictionary. "Ow we spake"*, and it is a cracking publication. Below are some of the words included by Steve.

Bawby – simpleton.
Bawk – confuse.
Bezum – broom or brush.
Caggyanded – left handed.
Core – cannot.
Clarnet – fool.
Cock-aiver – good punch.

Cog winder – good punch.
Cor – cannot in the singular.
Cort – cannot in the plural.
Cost – can you?
Day – did not.
Dobbin – little cart.
Fanaigue – not do as you promised.
Firkle – to mess about with.
Franzy – irritated.
Gammittin – playing the fool.
Gawby – fool.
Haiver – something large.
Jed – dead.
Jimmuckin – shaking.
Lezzer – meadow.
Lief – as soon as.
Lommock – large and clumsy.
Lungeous – boisterous.
Maunch – chew over carefully.
Mun – must.
Piece – slice of bread.
Riffy – very dirty.
Saided – is contented.
Spake – speak.
Spottle – splash.
Thee cosnt – You cannot.
Theirnun – belonging to them.
Thraerpe – good hiding.
Tocky bonk – pit mound.
Tranklements – small possessions.
Trussen – to trust.
Tunky – fat.
Umman – woman.
Wammel – animal, usually a dog.
Werriter – worrier.
Wum – home.
Yed – head.

Gis Thi Fist

Recently at a talk I gave at **Portobello Methodist Church, Willenhall**, Mary Wakelam recounted a marvellous saying that Grandmas would use when sending a child on an errand to the shop: "Gis thi fist, ere thi bist, off thi gust and mind the oss road". Another old phrase related to a couple having a covert affair and went "Them two an got fower elbers" (four elbows).

Ee cor tell Ay

Mr C. G. Smith of **Cotwall End Road, Lower Gornal** corrects me about the spelling of one of the sayings that I used recently. I had put "He do know A from a bull's foot". He tells me that it should be "E cor tell ay (hay) from a bull's foot", in other words a country bumpkin or someone who did not know a lot. Mr Smith has also sent me some Old Gornal sayings.

E wore oss turd igh – for someone rather small.

Stand a pike elm apart – keep your distance.

Ee's on orse an orse on eesen – he is on hers and she is on his, that is for a male riding a female bike and a female riding a male bike.

Arm a gooin up the wooden ill – going to bed.

Arm as code as a toad ice bound pule – I'm freezing.

Bomb damage at Avery's, Smethwick during the Second World War, hit despite the protection of the two sisters as described in Brian Dakin's poem.

A view of Cleveland Street, Wolverhampton from around the turn of the twentieth century, with the library at Snow Hill dominating the scene – near to where Ted, who contacted Carl about his concerns on pronunciations, once lived.

Liz Dickinson of **Cherry Tree Road, Kingswinford** feels that "the following is probably too modern, but I thought it would give you a 'good loff!' In 1967 I was a 21yr old Yorkshire lass, newly-wed and moved to the Midlands. I was working as a supply teacher at the Bluecoat School in Dudley and struggling to understand the Black Country dialect – and be understood by the pupils! Leaving school one evening I passed a couple of 1st year Asian girls by the gate and we wished each other a polite 'Good evening'. As I turned the corner, I heard one say to the other: 'Ay, D'yo think er's forrin?'"

Joyce C Aldridge from **Lonsdale Road, Park Hall, Walsall** recalls a few sayings from her childhood that were used by her parents, grandparents, aunts and uncles.

"A blind man on a gallopin oss wouldn't see it – about something that would go
    unnoticed.
Our cat went up your entry – referring to some tenuous link with a thing or person.
It'll end up in a cryin match – no good will come of it.
Keep out the oss road – keep out of trouble.

Up the wooden hill to Bedfordshire – time for bed.
A little help's worth a deal of pity – self explanatory.
Sturs – stairs.
Saft as a boiled owl – a very lenient, sensitive person.
Daft as a brush – self explanatory.
Triumphed again! – got it right."

A few years back, I was sent a thoughtful letter from a bloke called Ted of **Low Hill Wolverhampton** who was one my BBC WM listeners and who was concerned that radio station announcers and presenters were having an adverse impact on the way local words were pronounced. Then 73 he pointed out that "my accent and pronunciations are from my young days in the small streets at the back of the old Royal Hospital by the old Bus Depot (now gone) in Cleveland Street. This runs into the Bilston Road. May I say first Carl I was told to 'keep out the Hoss Road'. No horses by us, only Hosses. Now Carl the change of pronunciation in our area is I am sure caused by the newsreaders on WM radio. Before WM our name of Mander Shopping Centre now, but a paint works before that, well people from our area worked at Marnders not Manders. But readers of names use the non local accent or

The Royal Hospital, Wolverhampton, which was opened in 1849, seen in March 1961, and part of the district in which grew up one of Carl's listeners.

pronunciations. Here are a few from my memory. Wombourne – we say Wombun or Wumbun. Tettenhall – Tetnull. Brick Kiln Street – Bricklin. Shrewsbury not Shrowsbury. Nestle chocolate – Nesuls. Rowley not Rouley."

Place Names in Black Country Dialect

Amptun – Wolverhampton
Bilson – Bilston
Black Brook – the River Tame
Bramich or Bromich – West Bromwich
Brummagem – Birmingham
Carma – Caldmore
Cawzey Green – Causeway Green
Darlo – Darlaston
Hampton – Wolverhampton
Kiddie – Kidderminster
Netheren – Netherton
Odebury – Oldbury
Ode Ill – Old Hill
Quarry Bonk – Quarry Bank
Smerrick – Smethwick
Sturbridge – Stourbridge
Tettnull – Tettenhall
Tippun – Tipton
Yelse – Halesowen
Wedgebury – Wednesbury
Wedgefield or Wedgefoot – Wednesfield

Two Sisters

Brian Dakin, better known as Billy Spake Mon, of **Tower Road, Tividale** is a dialect poet of power, persuasion and intuition. I am convinced that his poetry will be amongst the most important of literary works to come out of the Black Country and the West Midlands. Talented, resourceful and infused with a love for our language, Billy has the ability to become as significant a poetic figure for our dialect as was Tennyson for Lincolnshire. A while ago Billy wrote to me about Bury Hill Park, which stretches from the Birmingham Road up across the Rowley Hills to meet Portway Hill and thence to Oakham and Dudley.

Billy declares that "the views from the top of Bury Hill are breathtaking, taking in the skyline of Birmingham and panning round to drown then eye in the beauty that is our Black Country. There are many stories connected with Bury Hill, the legend of Saint Brade being one, but here I will speak briefly about Big and Little Bertha who stood throughout the Second World War. Most of my knowledge comes from listening to stories at my Nan's house in Portway Road, Oldbury, so many of your readers will have a more detailed and accurate account. Of these sisters, Big and Little Bertha were in fact large cannons (I apologise to the technical experts), that were sited on the slopes of Bury Hill Park facing the town of my birth, Oldbury. Their purpose was to defend the town from the waves of German bombers that came and sought to destroy the factories in the valley below, whose purpose it was to produce ammunition and guns in double quick time for our soldiers at the front.

"The sight of the two sisters silhouetted against the strong sunlight or caught in the glare of the piercing searchlights gave the people of the town confidence that they would survive any onslaught from the enemy and the sound of them when they were deployed in defence was the greatest of battlecrys. Also, on a lighter note, there was many a photograph taken against the sisters of young women of the town and similar inscriptions as the ones my mother and aunts sent, 'to my darling love' written on the back and posted off to all corners of the globe in those long, long years of war."

Two Sisters

Two sisters stood on Bury 'Ill Bonk
As the bombers cum on in.
The fowke on Odebury luk up from the Markit Plairce
"Dow let the buggers win", Nelly Cradduck spakes.

They stond sow prowd defiyunt,
They'll omma these neckus, they wull,
Smosh un lomp um owt the sky
"They wow bully us, nar loff", Yung Tummy cries.

Agen the coledust sky
The sairchliytes puk um owt,
Fowke tuk thesen in the Andersen sheltus
"Dowt them lites now Polly" wus the cry.

The capstuns carry on rowlin
The wairkus kept the liyne
Jus liyke them ut the battlefront
"Sisters will win this time", they pray

Yow eye the echo on the shell fiya
Liyke the Baggis crowdus the team appeeya,
"Yow con cum us many a tiyme us yow want
Tew sisters will still be eya!"
Ode Bairty Milla luks up and sheks 'is fist.

Tew sisters stond on Bury 'Ill
The niyte silylunt agen,
Onny the rhythm on the peepuls arts
Stondin fairm fer when they cum next tiyme.

The sun brairks ova the brow 3 o'clock,
Wenchis dolled up theye ter the niynes
Sot on the sisters smile big us a buck oss
Sendin the messigis away down the liyne

Tew the wun thut ar luv tek this pitkcha
Owde it theya clowse ter yer 'art
Tew sisters wull keep us sairf frum 'arm
We wow eva part agen
My luv we wow eva part.

Chapter 13

BACK-TO-BACK AND UP
THE YARD. THE 1800s

Unprecedented population growth, mass migration, the rapid rise of manufacturing towns and the apparently sudden appearance of a class-based society transformed the look and feel of England irrevocably from the early 1800s. And at the forefront of these radical and astounding changes were Birmingham and the Black Country. Under the impetus of industrialisation, in the sixty years from 1821 the population of Birmingham exploded to 401,000, and similar remarkable increases were evident in the Black Country. In Bilston the populace grew from 12,000 in 1821 to 23,500 in 1851; between 1801 and 1861 the number of people in Dudley more than quadrupled from 10,107 to 44,975; in the decade from 1821, the folk of West Bromwich shot up from 5,822 to 15,377; and Wolverhampton's inhabitants burgeoned from just over 12,500 in 1801 to 60,860 in 1861. These towns were not alone in the expansion of their citizenry, for Tipton, Walsall, Sedgley, Kingswinford, Wednesbury, Oldswinford, Hales Owen, Darlaston, Rowley Regis, Willenhall and Wednesfield also swelled greatly in size.

With an unprecedented and seemingly insatiable demand for houses, the land-hungry towns of the West Midlands greedily grabbed the fields of nearby farms for development and overwhelmed as many open spaces within their boundaries as was possible. Gardens, allotments and plots of all kinds disappeared under the relentless onslaught of urbanisation led by jerry builders. Small-scale and short of funds, these builders sought ways to put as many houses as cheaply as possible on to as small a plot as possible and so maximise the return on their investment. Unhindered by planning regulations, in Birmingham and much of the Black Country they did this by throwing up back-to-back houses as quickly as they could.

Usually put up on impure foundations and built shoddily with inferior materials such as dirt instead of sand for the mortar, a back-to-back house was part of a terrace at the back of which was another house belonging to another terrace. Thus two houses shared a dividing wall merely one brick in depth, meaning that there were no back doors or windows. Consequently there was a lack of light and no through ventilation. All back-to-backs had a small room downstairs which was multi-purpose in its functions, having to serve as a living room, dining room, kitchen,

Number 15 Court, Adams Street, Duddeston, about 1905. Notice the whiteness of the pinnies of the woman and child and the clean curtains. The yard is blue-bricked and there is a maiding tub on the right. On the left, behind the gas lamp, you can just see the entry leading to the street.

wash room, work room and sometimes a bedroom. Cooking was on an open fire and later on a range, from which there was a jack upon which meat was hung to cook above the fire. A stewpot stood nearby, into which went any food not eaten and any bits left from preparing a meal.

Often there was a tiny scullery, in which in later years there would be a crock sink and a few shelves; and sometimes there was a cellar in which coal, slack and wood were kept for fuel. The flooring of the all-encompassing room downstairs was sometimes beaten earth or more commonly it was quarry tiles. This would be covered by peg rugs, made by bodging or podging (stitching) old rags on to urden sacking. Women worked determinedly at these rugs, trying to make attractive and colourful patterns. Many back-to-backs were two-storey high, meaning that there were two small bedrooms above the one room downstairs. However, there were a large number of attic high back-to-backs which gave extra sleeping space by having one bedroom above another.

Long terraces of back-to-backs dominated many streets. Between four or more of these front houses there was an entry which led to what officials called a court but which was known by working-class Brummies and Black Country folk as the yard or fode. This gave access to the houses behind the front houses and normally to another terrace of back-to-backs that ran along the yard. The houses that backed on to these faced into another yard. Each yard was shared space in which there were communal facilities. These included the brew'us, in which a copper was set in brick and below which there was space to light a fire.

Women would fill the copper with water, an arduous task in itself. Until the later nineteenth century water was drawn from polluted wells or taken from water butts, and even after significant improvements in public health provisions the women of each yard only had a shared standpipe. Buckets had to be filled with water and lugged into the brew'us and poured into the copper. It was hard collar keeping clean, because the women had to cart up to fifty gallons of water for a single wash of one boiling and rinsing.

From the early 1900s onwards, Lively Polly was added as a form of washing powder and once the copper was full, the fuel of slack, potato peelings and bits of wood could be lit. The dirty washing was dropped in and after it had been boiled up it was put into a maiding tub filled with water. Usually this was the larger part of a beer barrel. The women banged the washing about with a dolly or maid, a long and thick stick which had a cross-bar handle and a block of wood at the bottom. Then the clothes and bed linen were put in the scrubbing tub, the smaller part of the beer barrel, for rubbing strenuously on a scrubbing board.

The whites were now separated from the colours, swilled, boiled again in fresh water, swilled one more time and dipped into a bucket of water and Reckitt's Blue to give them a bluey whiteness. Anything that had to be starched, such as shirts, were put in a bucket of starch and all the washing was stretched through a mangle to get rid of much of the water. Many's a girl has had a finger injured in turning the mangle for her mom, or has caught her long hair in it. After mangling, the washing was pegged out to dry – in the yard if it were fine, but in the one downstairs room if it were not.

Next some of the water from the boiler was once more put into buckets and bowls, for the soaking of heavily stained clothing. What water that was left would be fetched into the house. Here the woman would climb the steep stairs and then chuck down the water so that she might scrub clean the wooden stairs and floor downstairs. Finally, the dried washing was ironed with a flat iron, for the making of

Women working in a yard of two-storey and attic high back-to-backs off William Street, about 1905.

which West Bromwich was world famed. This was another long and laborious task. For so many women, the heavy chore of washday was carried on by the light of spluttering candle of a night time, after they had finished their industrial work; whilst for others, the hardship of their own washing was exacerbated by having to take in the washing of the better off so as to earn a few coppers.

The brew'us and the shared well and later standpipe were amongst a number of communal facilities. Each yard would have an area for the ashes and rubbish – although anything that could be recycled was used again in some way. In Birmingham and much of the Black Country this spot was called the miskins and later that word was applied to the dustbins which were put into the yards. Derived from the Anglo-Saxon word mixen meaning dung, miskins came to be used for the dung heap in a village. Its survival into the twentieth century in an urban and industrial setting highlights how ancient words rooted in the rural past were brought into the manufacturing towns of the West Midlands by rural incomers from South Staffordshire, North Warwickshire and North Worcestershire. In this way, the back-to-back folk of the Black Country and Brummagem were bonded with the Angles

Women washing in the tumbledown brew'us in a yard off Bishopsgate Street, close to Broad Street. The dolly or maid is in the maiding tub closest to the washing on the line. The figures of the women and children on the left are blurry because they are moving slightly, and the cameras of the day were too slow to focus on people moving.

who had settled in our region as far back as the early 500s; and they handed to us wonderfully expressive phrases like 'marry the miskin for the money and get pizened by the stink on it'.

Close to the miskins were the lavatories. In the early years of yards, the lavatory was usually a communal privy or cess pit which overflowed so that offensive matter flowed into the wells dirtying them and making the water unhealthy and dangerous to drink. It is little wonder that water-borne diseases so preyed upon working-class folk. Occasionally, the cess pits were emptied by the night soil men. When they did so, horrid and noxious smells pervaded the atmosphere. The vile conditions of so many yards were made plain in William Lee's *Report* on the sewage, drainage, supply of water and sanitary condition of Dudley in 1852. Lee stated that in Vane's Yard off Birmingham Street, one privy was shared by the residents of seven houses and lodging houses. The newly-constructed Pudding Bag Street in the town was as bad. Unpaved and undrained, it had no piped water supply or standpipe and its cess pools were stagnant and filthy.

For the poor of these streets and others like them, clean water was an expensive they could not afford. Following the cholera epidemic of 1832, the Dudley Water Works Company was set up to bring in fresh water from wells at Hurst Hill and Parkes Hall and a reservoir at Shavers End. Unhappily, only the wealthy could buy the water, given that a supply cost between nine shillings (45 pence) and £3 a year. This was at a time when many families had to make do on an income of less than £1 a week.

Still even those who were comfortably off could suffer the wretched consequences of an absence of drains and sewers. Samuel Cooke was a draper in King Street and a leader of the Dudley Chartists. In 1852, he complained of the want of a proper sewer to his house and that "the drainage is all along the surface. In winter the filth is often frozen. In my house . . . we have a cesspool and carry the liquid refuse out in buckets, emptying them on the surface of the back yard". Conditions were even worse in Packwood's Buildings in Fisher Street, Dudley. Here twenty back-to-back houses shared four privies which were filthy and reeked vilely.

John Houghton was a surgeon who had practised for eleven years in the town. He told Lee that on occasions his work brought him into contact with poorer inhabitants. Their dwellings struck him as incompatible with health. They were located in badly constructed lanes, alleys, streets and courts in which ventilation was impossible. He went on:

> I have frequently broken panes out of windows to let in a little air, many will not open, and in almost innumerable instances the cottages are built back-to-back, so that there can be no draught of air . . . in multitudes of cases there are windows with privies under them . . . so foul that they cannot be used; they often have soil-pits, often full of semi-liquid ordure . . . The courtyards are unpaved, some entirely; others have a channel or a footpath of rough stones or bricks and this is often dilapidated . . . I consider these evils surrounding the dwellings of the poor are sufficient causes of excessive disease and mortality existing in Dudley.

Matters were no better in Wolverhampton, where back-to-backs and small cottages crowded the older, central localities such as Stafford Street, Walsall Street, Salop Street and Carribee Island. A host of narrow alleyways and overcrowded yards like Outmeal Square ran off and behind these streets. In 1841 an observer reported with distaste that stagnant pools, "the colour of dead porter, with a glistening metallic film over them" were in the front of the houses in Stafford Street. Sometimes these pools resembled "a sort of disgusting mixture of gruel and soap suds. After a day's rain many of them have a little pond in front, the size of a quilt, the colour of liquorice tea."

Eight years later, Robert Rawlinson inquired into the sewerage, drainage and water supply of Wolverhampton, noting that in the poorer parts of the town the privies and ash pits "are open tanks, or receptacles for the soil, which is afterwards covered over until full with fire ashes and other refuse. In very many instances the privies have been built over the ancient ditches or watercourses, leaving their contents openly exposed until some heavy falls of rain shall wash away the same, and where such is the caser we seldom find any ashpits at all; the consequence is that an accumulation of ashes etc. finds its way into the same reservoir, and the whole becomes a mass of stagnated corruption." Little wonder that in Wolverhampton the life expectancy was nineteen years and one month, compared to thirty-seven years and nine months in Penkridge just to the north. The infant mortality rate, especially, was horrendous, with one in six Wulfrunian babies dying before they were one.

The poor of Birmingham lived in as bad an environment, as Rawlinson made plain in another report in 1849. In many yards the water was drawn from wells that were "impregnated with offensive matter" flowing in from uncleansed streets, overfull cesspits, sodden miskins and crammed graveyards. Most of these yards were closed in on all sides, with the communal privies and cesspools crowded against them. The air was heavy and stank. The disgusting odours and noxious substances were made worse by the 336 butchers of the town, large numbers of whom had their private slaughter-houses hard and fast to houses. Pig sties and heaps of manure gave off more unpleasant smells.

In 1875, Dr Hill, Birmingham's Medical Officer of Health drew attention to the awful difference between the death rates between rich and poor. In wealthy Edgbaston 13.11 died per thousand people. By comparison the general mortality rate in Saint Mary's Ward (the Gun Quarter around Saint Chad's Cathedral) was twice as much at 26.82. Between ten and twelve thousand people lived in the ward and their dreadful environment was called forth by William White, a respected Quaker and Liberal councillor. Many of the dwellings locally were dilapidated; their floors were damp; and they suffered from the oozing of filth through the walls "causing horrible stenches".

Conditions such as these in Dudley, Wolverhampton, Birmingham and elsewhere led to calls for action. Public health campaigners advocated that each town should have powers to enforce and implement public health provisions. They argued that it was essential for the well being of the nation that working-class people were healthier so that they could become more efficient workers. This utilitarian attitude was leavened by Christian concern and humanitarianism and also

A mother and her children chopping firewood in their back-to-back. These photos are from my book Homes For People. Council Housing and Urban Renewal in Birmingham 1840-1999 (Brewin Books, 1999).

by the awareness that the diseases that flourished in poorer areas because of non-existent or inadequate public health facilities could spread to the middle class. Gradually, the campaigners made headway and authorities began to emerge with responsibilities for sewers, drains, fresh water supplies, street cleansing, the removal of nuisances and housing bye-laws.

From 1853, Dudley was covered by a Board of Health and its officers began to alert the owners of back-to-backs as to the bad state of their property – something most were unaware of because they received their rent from paid collectors. Orders were made for the cleansing and whitewashing of the most insanitary houses, but in many parts of the town affairs remained appalling. In Gate House Yard, Birmingham Street fifty-two people lived in eight houses and shared two "putrescent privies". The drains were blocked and there was no water supply.

From 1865, the powers of the Board of Health were held by the new town council, but the poor continued to die earlier and in greater numbers – as they did throughout the West Midlands. In 1871, a report emphasised the high rate of typhus in Dudley and the inadequacy and insufficiency of sewers and drains. Three years later it was revealed that 20% of houses still took water from polluted wells. Proper sewers, drains and fresh waters did not begin to make their mark in Dudley until the 1880s and afterwards. Even then, little attention was paid to the bad condition of the back-to-backs in the wards of Saint Thomas and Saint Edwards. These were not cleared by the Council until the 1920s and 1930s, when their people were moved to the Priory and Wren's Nest estates. Wolverhampton acted more quickly in doing away with bad property, clearing the North Street, Carribee Island and Berry Street neighbourhood in the late nineteenth century. Unfortunately, officials made no provision for those who had lost their homes and so the poor moved into the adjoining quarters where overcrowding became more pronounced.

The same unfortunate phenomenon was evident in Birmingham. Under the dynamic mayor, Joseph Chamberlain, the building of back-to-backs was banned in 1876 and from the late 1870s to the end of the nineteenth century, hundreds of houses were demolished to make way for the cutting of Corporation Street. Thousands of poor folk were made homeless. Desperate for somewhere to live they pushed into the already overcrowded area around Gosta Green.

As the twentieth century dawned, 200,000 Brummies still lived in back-to-backs. That was a city the size of Salford or Cardiff. Tens of thousands continued to live in back-to-backs until the end of the 1960s. Despite their bad conditions a strong community spirit characterised the back-to-back neighbourhoods of Brummagem and the Black Country.

Chapter 14

BACK TO LIFE AND THE REALITY
OF CROWDING IN A TINY SPACE

Back-to-back and up the yard was the lived experience of hundreds of thousands of Black Country folk and Brummies from the early years of the 1800s to the late 1960s. Small, usually badly built and tightly-packed on to small plots of land, back-to-back houses were common across Wolverhampton, the Black Country, Birmingham and much of the north of England. Dark, lacking in through ventilation, cramped and with communal privies (later dry pan privies and then water closets), shared wells (later stand-pipes) and common miskins, back-to-backs soon drew the attention of concerned commentators. As early as 1840, the Select Committee on the Health of Towns, headed by the MP for Shrewsbury, Robert Slaney, called for a general building act that would apply to certain classes of houses where experience showed that sanitary regulations were essential. This would forbid the building of back-to-backs and of houses in courts and alleyways without a thoroughfare at each end. A bill to that end was introduced. It failed, falling upon the rock of a Parliament that was dominated by property owners who resented any suggestion that their rights should be infringed. Thus the rights of the poor were sacrificed for the motive of quick profits from bad housing.

Recognising the need for better quality homes for the working class and that builders would not provide them unless enjoined to do so, Manchester banned the building of back-to-backs in 1844. Its example was later followed by Liverpool, but in Birmingham back-to-backs were built until 1876 when a bye-law effectively forbade them. In parts of the Black Country they continued to appear for a few more years, as they did in Balsall Heath, which did not join Birmingham until 1891, and Aston, which came within the city in 1911. Finally in 1909, a town planning act banned the building of back-to-backs nationally. In Leeds, however, they continued to be put up until the 1930s because builders had put in numerous applications before the Act was passed and had gained planning approval. Today there are over 30,000 in that city.

Built hard and fast by factories, in neighbourhoods where the light was dowted and the fresh air was sullied by the pollution of industry and the crowding together of buildings, back-to-backs were embedded in a gloomy setting and were blackened by the smoke that was belched out by innumerable factories and works. Outsiders shrank from such neighbourhoods, offended by the pungent odours, the lack of privacy, the darkness and the harsh sounds of manufacturing. In 1901, J. Cuming Walters stirred up the environment of back-to-back Birmingham for the readers of the *Daily Gazette*.

The air is heavy with a sooty smoke and with acid vapours, and here it is the poor live – and wither away and die. How do they live? Look at the houses, the alleys, the courts, the ill-lit, ill-paved, walled-in squares, with last night's rain still trickling down from the roofs and making pools in the ill-sluiced yards. Look at the begrimed windows, the broken glass, the apertures stopped with yellow paper or filthy rags; glance in at the rooms where large families eat day and sleep every night and every night, amid rags and vermin, within dank and mildewed walls from which the blistered paper is drooping, or the bit of discolouration called "paint" is peeling away. Here you can veritably taste the pestilential air, stagnant and nephitic, which finds no outlet in the prison-like house of the courts; and yet here, where there is breathing-space for so few, the many are herded together, and

Young girls playing in a yard off Icknield Port Road, Ladywood in the later 1960s. Notice the entry in the background and the shared lavatories and brew'us on the right.

overcrowding is the rule not the exception. The poor have nowhere else to go. It is here, amid the rank and rotting garbage, in the filthy alleys and within the time-blackened old-fashioned dwellings, near the ill-smelling canal, or in the vicinage of factories which pour out their fumes in billowing masses from the throat of giant stacks – here it is they must come for shelter.

Walters's powerful writing reaches out yet to us, and many other reports confirmed that back-to-back living killed the poor. In 1898, Dr Alfred Hill, Birmingham's first Medical Officer of Health, carried out an investigation into the city's 43,366 back-to-backs, many of which were grouped into 6,000 yards. It revealed that most of these dwellings were rented at 3s 6d a week (17½p). In Saint Bartholomew's Ward, now the Eastside redevelopment area of Digbeth between Moor Street Station and Millennium Point, over half of the houses were of this type and the annual death rate was 32.7 per thousand people. In areas with no such houses, the death rate was dramatically lower at 17.1. Each year because of poor quality, unhygienic back-to-backs, 3,000 people died who would have lived given better housing. The infant mortality was even more dreadful. Overall this was twice as great as in certain

A young lad shins up a lamp-post on the corner of Bridge Street West, Hockley, Birmingham in the mid-1960s.

smaller towns and rural districts, but such a general statistic shrouded even worse figures. The highest rate was in Saint Stephen's Ward, which covered part of Hockley and the Summer Lane neighbourhood, and where back-to-backs were also plentiful. Three times as many infants under one died here as in wealthy Edgbaston and Harborne. The conclusion was inescapable. There was a close connection between the infant mortality rate and the housing conditions.

It was recognised that there was also bad housing in the countryside, but the scale of the problem in the urbanised West Midlands was so great that it magnified the difficulties of jerry-built structures. Most back-to-backs had damp floors downstairs because the quarries were laid on the bare earth. The walls were also full of moisture because they did not have a damp course, and the brickwork, pointing and spouting was defective. As a result of the dampness, the woodwork was decayed and rotten. Furthermore, the surfaces of the walls and ceilings were not smooth and hard and so accumulated dirt and dust. The reports of Dr Hill and Dr Robertson in Birmingham reinforced surveys such as that of Dr Edward Ballard in Dudley in 1874. This emphasised the dire problems facing those who lived in back-to-backs. Shared privies were often full to the seat, leading residents to relieve themselves on the ground. In June of that year, 108 people applied for the council to remove sewage, but only six had their request attended to. In Number One Court, Newhall Street in Saint Thomas's Ward, one pump well supplied seven houses. Its water was contaminated by polluted sub-soil. Overall, Dudley's back-to-backs were damp and dirty and stood in unpaved and undrained yards "with slops standing in pools or running uncontrolled over the surface of the ground". In Birmingham Street, a woman reported that the ash pit of a property to the rear of her house drained into her pantry. This ash pit was also the receptacle of human refuse. There are few working-class testimonies from the nineteenth and early twentieth centuries and fewer still that give an insider's view of back-to-back houses.

One of them is that of Will Thorne. From a poverty-stricken family, Thorne went on to found the Gasworkers' Union and become a celebrated trade unionist. In his life story he relates how he was born "in a little four-roomed house" in Farm Street, Hockley, "but I have no memories of the free air of a farm during those early far-off days; just the ugly houses and cobbly, neglected streets that were my only playground for a few short, very short years". V. W. Garratt was born in a similarly poor part of Birmingham in 1892. His yard in the Holloway Head district had a communal water tap, the wells having been closed a few years earlier, and two wash-houses that were backed by a dust pit (ash pit) into which was emptied the refuse of the two adjoining closets. The yard was paved with brick and so "it was possible to tell by the familiar footsteps who was going in or out without drawing aside of curtains. Life could not be lived unto itself in those small communities."

A yard in the Summer Lane neighbourhood in the 1930s.

Our own household was pressed into one small living-room, where we jostled each other with the restless abandon of children, while in the same atmosphere was done the cooking, the bathing, the eating, and the clothes-mending to a never-ending din of voices. A perilous flight of stairs led to the bedroom overhead, and higher still was the gloomy attic, crowned by chimney pots. The slated roof was seldom free from dislocations. Adjoining the living room was a small, dark pantry with a brick sink at the one end and the cellar steps at the other. The cellar was the special preserve of my father, for it was his practice to store up in it a reserve supply of coal . . .

As for fixtures and furnishings, these were of the simplest and consisted of a table, chairs, a chiffonier, old couch, a well-used sewing machine and a oil-lamp hanging from the ceiling. Upstairs, the bedroom of Garratt's parents had an iron bedstead, a table with a detachable mirror, a small chair with a matted seat half torn out, and an old wooden box covered with wallpaper. The eight children slept four to a bed in the attic.

More recently, the lives of those whose address was back of have been brought to the fore by Kathleen Dayus in her intuitive book, *Her People* (Virago: 1982). Kathleen Dayus knew what it was to rough it. The thirteenth child of a poor family, she grew up in a yard in Camden Street on the edge of the Jewellery Quarter. In one of the most prosperous cities of one of the wealthiest counties in the world, the local folk had to collar and scrat for everything and anything they had. Like Kathleen's dad, many of the chaps were out of work and were on the parish, "but what they received was insufficient to feed us growing children, let alone our parents as well". On Friday afternoons, the hard up and unemployed would queue for cards that allowed them a bit of coal, a loaf or two, some margarine, a tin of condensed milk, a little tea, and a spoonful or so of sugar. This relief was grudging and meagre and money was never given. In their prejudice against the poor, too many of those in authority believed that poorer folk could not be trusted with cash in case they spent it on snuff, tobacco, beer or suchlike.

Poverty was a hard bed. Kathleen and her pals knew what it was to be clammed and to stand outside the factory gates begging for a piece off the workers when they knocked off. And they knew what it was like to live in tiny houses that were badly built and to have to share insanitary dry-pan closets. As if that was not enough, Kathleen was treated harshly by her mom. She was a tough woman who would bounce out of the house with the old mon's flat cap pushed firmly onto her head. In later years, Kathleen came to an understanding of why her mom was that way. It was life that had squeezed the affection from her and made her forbidding.

But the life that Kathleen and her pals lived was not one of unremitting unhappiness. They had their laughs, they played their games, they whistled and they sang and they made the best of the bed that they lay on. Outsiders, no matter how well meaning, were oblivious to these features. Nor were they able to grasp the resilience of those who lived in the back streets and of how they forged energetic and successful neighbourhoods. Lacking back gardens and often with just a tint patch of land for a front garden, the people of back-to-back Brummagem and the Black Country lived as much in the street as they did in their homes – if not more so. This

Women washing in a tumbledown brew'us in Hanley Street in the 1930s.

Coronation Day celebrations in Milton Street, Summer Lane in 1953.

characteristic transformed each street into a living thing, brought into being by its people who canted on the street, played in the street, walked along the street, met in the street and watched the goings on of the street. A vital entity, the street's power and vigour were enhanced by corner shops where mothers gathered to shop, exchange information and pass on the news of the locality, and by small, local pubs. These acted as leisure centres with their fishing, dominoes, cribbage and football clubs; as bases for mutual benefit societies such as the Buffs; and as focal points for the celebrations and mourning of families, the community and the nation. Then there were the mission halls and small chapels that provided youngsters with instructions in Christian values through Sunday School and which organised outings up the cut on the coal boat, and which served as another essential place for the gathering of the local folk.

Of course there were rows and fights; that is not surprising when so many were packed so closely together. And there were those whose principles and life-styles fell below the high standard set by the great majority, but what is most remarkable is that so many strove so hard to maintain their dignity and respectability and that of their families. In their determination to live decently and be good neighbours, the folk of the back streets serve as compelling examples in a modern world in which the street has been grabbed by yobs and in which neighbourliness is no longer pushed forward as a positive concept. The back-to-back folk belonged to "we" and "us" neighbourhoods and not to a "me" and "I" world. Living amidst extended family and kin and alert to the importance of giving to others because it was the right thing to do, they grew up with the unconscious understanding that there was a need to share.

Selfishness and individualism had no place in neighbourhoods where communal and collective actions were so important. Each street had an old lady who laid out the dead and who brought babies in to the world, a woman who was a wise woman, another who collected the money for the street parties and charabanc trips, and wenches who were physically strong and would soon bring someone into line if they was playing up and flouting the codes of conduct. In such streets Our Mom and Our Gran were the key figures, instilling rules of behaviour, helping out younger family members, passing on the tales of the past, and drawing the kin together.

Few today would mourn the clearance of back-to-back and other bad housing, but paradoxically in demolishing the unwanted housing legacy of the Victorian age we destroyed neighbourhoods that had taken years to emerge as settled communities. History does not teach us exact lessons. The context of time and place shifts too quickly and effectively to make that possible. But what history can do is give us pointers as to how we might change society for the better, just as our own personal experiences can inform for the good our decisions about our lives. Perhaps the most important pointer is this: we owe a debt to those who endured insanitary conditions, bad housing, diseases, early deaths and hardships a plenty, and if we are to repay that debt we should seek to take note of the example of how they created strong neighbourhoods in the most unfavourable of environments. The back-to-back folk did not and do not ask us for sympathy, but they do deserve our respect and a prominent place in our history.

Chapter 15

TIN SHOP YARD AN' ALL THAT

Geoff Brown has heeded well the tales of his family. Intent upon ensuring that neither these stories nor their tellers should be forgotten, Geoff has written down what he could remember in an insightful book called *Tin Shop Yard 'an all that*. In the main, it is an account of incidents in the life of his uncle, Harry, which were recited to Geoff when Harry was in his seventies. Mindful that they may have been commonplace stories, still Geoff felt rightly that they were worth preserving "if only to make us count our blessings and give thanks for better times, instead of bemoaning our minor and easily surmountable problems".

With a clarity of understanding for his people and their lives and a deep sympathy for their lot that is tinted neither by sentimentality or wistfulness, Geoff stresses that "it is a sad feature of most lives that when we reach the end of our lives we are surrounded by folk who never knew us at our best. The brave young warrior is invisible to those who see the bent old man, and the ravishing young beauty is rarely visible behind the grey haired old lady. And yet the end of every life is to close the book on an epic adventure.

"Each and everyone of us has worked and fought to live and fulfil our ambitions. The best we can claim is that we fought hard and not wasted too much precious time. Anyone who has done that has a story worth telling and this is a small part of the story of one Wolverhampton family and their struggles. They may have been a family like yours, in fact your family may well have known them or lived nearby. They would certainly have walked the same streets, shopped at the same shops, attended the same schools and churches and had very similar experiences."

The strength and vitality of Geoff's work lies in the way in which his family stories relate not only to the Browns and to those who lived in and around Stafford Street, but also to all those who endured poverty knocking daily at their door. Those who read Geoff's considered and perceptive words may not have walked the same streets, shopped at the same shops, and attended the same schools and churches but they may have walked the same kind of streets, shopped at the same kind of shops, and attended the same kind of schools and churches. Their experiences of life and its struggles would have been similar, irrespective of whether they lived in a yard in Wolverhampton, Brummagem, Tipton, Cradley Heath, Walsall, or The Lyng in West

Bromwich. For the power of Geoff's writing lies in its bond with the lives of poor working-class people across the Black Country and Birmingham and indeed across England, Ireland, Scotland and Wales.

Crucially, Geoff has also recognised the value of the spoken word in the telling of our history and the lack of simplicity in reaching out to the past. As he stresses, "in the course of family and local history research certain constants soon established themselves. One of them is that while witness, either written or spoken, is often changed or exaggerated by constant telling, it is hardly ever invented. Any story told will have a sound basis somewhere. The truth, when found, may be a bit disappointing but just as often it is more astonishing and intriguing than the tradition.

"Another constant is that everyone's view of events and people differ from any others. Even momentous and dramatic events will have many differing versions. The telling of day to day events will vary considerably in different generations. The

The Tin Shop Yard. The land framed on the right had cheap houses upon it. This photo was taken by the late Mr M. G. Copper of the Wolverhampton Photographic Society. I thank Mr J. Dowdall of the Society and the Society for allowing me to use it.

The 'Plume of Feathers' in North Street, with Granny Mattox next door outside her house. Granny Mattox was the mother of Geoff's Granny S'Ran and was essential in helping S'Ran through her life of hardship. Kin were the first and foremost allies of the poor in their never-ending fight against the tyranny of poverty. Thanks to Wolverhampton Archives and Local Studies.

man who was a tough, drunken and terrifying horror to his eldest daughter or son, may be a generous and benign delight to his youngest grandchild. Neither view is wholly right or wrong. The old man is neither as black or as white as memories paint him. Both witnesses would be amazed and offended if their versions were questioned, and quite rightly so because both versions were fair comment at the time. The truth lies in knowing it all, and we can never know that."

As Geoff stresses, we all see our past and that of our family through the looking glass of our own experiences, prejudices and beliefs. On occasions that looking glass fastens on something, bringing it into focus and making it clear to us if not to someone else who was there with us. Sometimes the focus may be blurred and only a misty memory emerges, or else the remembered happening may be magnified too much and made too big a thing or understated too much and made too little a thing.

And then again, the looking glass may not fasten upon many aspects of our past and leave them packed away in a deep recess of our mind never to be uncovered.

But whatever we recall, and in what manner we do so, it is crucial not only for our personal history but also for that of our families, our neighbourhoods, our region and our country. For too long our people were hidden from history, blanked out by the sources that fastened upon the rich and mighty and that ignored the poor, women, the disabled and others, except to demean them. Thank God that men and women like Geoff Brown have not bowed down to the enormous arrogance of this biased approach.

In writing down their family histories and bringing into view their people, our people, they have made as potent a contribution to democracy and the rights of working people as did the chainmaking wenches who fought for better pay and all those who strove to gain the vote for all adult men and women irrespective of their class, their creed and their colour. Every right gained by the working class was won at a cost by working-class folk and it redounds to us to honour our debt to those that fought for a better world to live. Let us not pass them by. Let us do what Geoff has done and make sure they are remembered in all their complexities – the good and the bad, the honourable and the dishonourable, the responsible and the irresponsible.

So, to Geoff's family. His uncle, Harry Brown, was born in 1900 in The Pleck, Walsall, the son of John, a horseshoe striker, and Sarah Ann, who was known as S'Ran. He had four brothers, Bill, Jack, Jim and Arthur, and one sister, Lottie. In their early years they led lives of considerable poverty. In the case of their family the misfortunes that befell them were "due to the apparent inability of their father, John Brown, to face up to his responsibilities. He frequently left home and Sarah Ann (often pregnant) to fend for the family".

Harry's reminiscences emphasise how important the mother was in working-class households, especially poorer working-class families. She it was who commanded the finances and

Harry Brown before joining up in 1918.

who was invested so often with the task of making the limited family income like a piece of elastic, stretching it as far as was possible. She it was who maintained her family's self-sufficiency through careful housekeeping and creative cooking. And she it was who made valiant efforts to stay clean and respectable. Often earning her own income and receiving the earnings of her children, it was the mother who was in charge of the daily battle against hunger and hardships.

Although born on The Pleck, Harry's first memories were of a small house in Molyneux Fold and of a yard "surrounded by low quality houses which were situated in front of the Molyneux Hotel. These houses were later demolished and replaced by a bowling green which was immediately in front of the hotel during the 1920s and 1930s. This, too, was replaced in later years by the existing car park."

Molyneux Fold was not on its own. As the assiduous research of Anthony Perry has shown, in Wolverhampton the name fold was given to many of the access-ways between buildings, at the backs of buildings and at the sides of buildings. These folds were not streets or thoroughfares in the accepted sense of

Sarah Ann Brown, S'Ran, with her granddaughter in the 1940s. Geoff's book, which is not generally available, is dedicated to his 'Grandmother, Sarah Ann Brown for her courage, kindness and unfailing generosity under all conditions".

the words and usually were footways that were too narrow for the passage of vehicles. The word fold itself harks back to the time when Wolverhampton was a leading centre of the wool trade nationally and sheep were penned in folds in the town. Elsewhere in the Black Country, the term sheep fold became the fode, the yard of a house.

When Harry Brown was still little, the family moved from Molyneux Fold to the Tin Shop Yard. As Geoff describes it, this was "a short, narrow road, almost an alley, running from North Road, opposite where the Fox pub still stands, to Charles Street. This in turn ran into Stafford Street. If you stood with your back to the Fox in those days, a row of small shops and businesses would have presented themselves, running away to the right of Tin Shop Yard towards the Chequer Ball which overlooked the Market Square and Saint Peter's.

"But back to the Tin Shop Yard. As you walked through North Street, towards Charles Street, the Yard rose fairly steeply uphill and had high boards on the right-hand side which were the boundary of factory and shop areas. On the left were the old, poor quality houses in which Harry lived. He can recall the door which led directly from the pavement into the one and only downstairs room. There was no rear entrance. Inside there was a large open range and a tap under which stood a small tin bath to catch the constant drips. It was very sparsely and poorly furnished with chairs without upholstery and a scrubbed-topped wooden table. From this room the stairs led to a single room above, the family's only sleeping accommodation. There was no cooker, just an open fire. No lighting system, only a paraffin lamp.

"For toilet facilities it was necessary to leave the house and walk along Tin Shop Yard to the top corner where a gate led to an open, communal yard containing several tin pans. These were the facilities for the families of the Tin Shop yard. The tins were emptied from time to time by men employed by the Council but as this service was a bit erratic, the tins would be frequently overflowing. Little

Geoff Brown in a pram in his yard in Stanhope Street, 1926.

The rear of the Brown's house in Stanhope Street. Richard Ling is seated and is holding Geoff, whilst Billy Cotterill is standing. Richard served with the Lincolnshire Regiment on the Khyber Pass in the 1930s and 1940s, while Billy was a parachute trooper in the Second World War and was captured by the enemy at Arnhem.

imagination is needed to visualise what an unpleasant place this was, as with no roof users would see the seasons change, from the smell and flies of high summer to the freezing cold of winter. The thought of coping with illness and colic when this was your only convenience – well, perhaps, I'd best not dwell on that. These privies were to be found in other parts of the area and could be located by anyone 50 yards to windward. I'm told they were also the reason for the deep breath and hurried walk of passers-by!

"Nearly all the houses of this area were owned by private landlords. Harry recalls the names of Kelly and Oliver being mentioned. It's doubtful if any of these landlords made much money from the very poor properties and the collection of the rents from these, the poorest inhabitants of the town, was one long struggle. In consequence the houses were continually changing hands as disillusioned owners sold to some stalwart who fancied himself harder or more cunning than his predecessor.

"Although the area may seem small now, at the time it contained thousands of small houses. These mingled with shops, lodging houses, factories, stables and pubs – lots of pubs – to form a variety of paths from one area to another. These were useful to Harry and other youngsters who could leap nimbly over the odd wall and squeeze through a fence or two. To strangers it was a frightening and mysterious place because quite a few rare characters resided there.

"It needs considerable effort these days to imagine the crowded closeness of the dirt streets and blue-brick pavements, with alleyways and entries disappearing into places unknown except to those who lived and worked there. The confusing maze, coupled with the belligerent, close and secretive manner which existed between the inhabitants of the courts, streets and yards resulted in an environment in which it was easy for people to move home and temporarily lose themselves."

Geoff explains that his grandmother, S'Ran, whom he knew well, had rarely lived in a house with running water and had never lived in a house with a cooker, a sink, a separate flush toilet, separate rubbish bins or any gas and electricity

Geoff today.

137

until she was nearly 60 years of age. He goes on to stress that "the area described in these stories had none of these things, and although these conditions produced some tough and unique characters, and countless families managed to live clean and civilised lives there, it was in truth, a horrible place to live. I should not like you to think that the humour which I hope you will find in these pages in any way masks the awfulness of the conditions.

"When I was interviewing the dozen or so ex-residents of the area, in search of background, I often expressed a desire to give a fair picture of the area and not to exaggerate the grimness of it all. Every one of these people responded without a second's hesitation by saying, 'You won't do that Geoff because it's impossible. Nothing could possibly exaggerate the horror of having to live in that place.' When I was not long married in 1950, the local authority began the final stages of demolition of Deanery Row and the many other streets, alleyways and yards which made up this grim place.

"Its end was planned by men of vision and it heralded a new world, which despite all its draw-backs, is infinitely better than that which it replaced. It is difficult now to see where all those streets and houses were; but make no mistake, Wolverhampton is better off without them."

Chapter 16

BACK-TO-BACK IN EBENEZER STREET

Barry Harper of **Aldridge** was moved to write to me following the articles on Back-to-Back Memories. He was "born in June 1949, in the 'Hallam' Hospital, West Bromwich. And then it was time to go home. Ebenezer Street, (you don't get names like that now), Hill Top. Although it was a back-to-back, all Mom and Dad had was the downstairs front room. (Sounds like a Monty Python sketch.) Apparently, I spent my first few months sleeping in a draw from the chest of drawers, used as a cot.

"I remember the back yard. Thinking about it, if we had the front of the house, to get to the yard, we must have had to go out into the street and up the entry. Must have been great in the middle of the night, especially in the winter. I remember the 'brewhouse' . . . And the big boiler. Meant nothing then of course. Looking back, everyone knew everyone else. At the top of the street, on the corner was a shop. Very dark, with lots of wood. I remember being lifted up onto the counter, and seeing the bacon machine. A big red thing.

"Dad was a bus conductor. I remember his big black metal box that he used to keep his ticket machine in. The box had a combination padlock on it. Fascinated me, that did. And his lapel badge. A big round thing. Green around the edge, and his number in the middle. Began with 'DD'. Whenever I see an old bus driver, wearing one of those badges, I always think of Dad. Dad's Brother, Bill, lived around the corner in the other part of Ebenezer Street, with Auntie Annie. And down on the bottom of Ebenezer Street, where it joined Dial Lane, was the 'Brit' (Britannia) pub.

"The story goes . . . that Uncle Bill was a comedian, who worked the local pubs and clubs. He had two main routines. One was where he came out dressed as a Boy Scout, complete with a jam jar full of toddlers. The other routine was that he came out dressed as a Vicar. Apparently, one Sunday morning, there was a coach party, must have been from distant parts that came to the Brit. One of the Sunday morning runs that they don't seem to do now.

"One of our family has a photo taken at the 'Boat' pub, in Lea Brook, which was taken just before the lads went on one of those Sunday morning runs. There's Dad, and his brothers-in-law and some other chaps. All wearing smart suits and hats. They looked like a bunch of gangsters.

"Anyway, back to the plot . . . There was a young couple in the bar of the 'Brit', who said they were going to get married soon. One of the regulars said that Reverend Harper could marry them there and then. They bought it. Someone went around to Uncle Bill's, and he arrived in the pub, in his Vicar's costume. The locals all went along with it, even down to the point where everyone was singing hymns, and he 'married' the couple in the bar. After which the Groom bought everyone in the pub a drink. It was only when the coach was pulling away from the pub that someone told them the truth. And Reverend Harper was nowhere to be found.

"I remember being in the kitchen at Gran's in Lea Brook, Wednesbury, when my Auntie Elsie came in and said 'The King's dead.' I remember at home in Ebenezer Street, Mom and Dad putting paper tape on the windows, it was striped red, white and blue. Must have been for the Coronation. I seem to recall one night being taken to the end of the street, to Dial Lane, and an illuminated bus came past. There were lots of people standing around, and it must have been for the Festival of Britain . . . Which would have been 1952?

"Going away from 'Back-to-Back' life, I was at Gran's one day when the family was putting crepe paper (red white and blue) around a flagpole in the hall. This must have been for the Coronation too. Grandad was there (what a man) and that was when Auntie Elsie sat on the drawing pins that were on the stairs . . .

"Grandad, (Mom's Dad) was Joseph Sillwood, also known as 'Dirky' because he collected knives (Dirks) and penknives. Grandad was a boatman. And a local legend. He would be away for a few days at a time on his boat. We went to meet him once, up on the 'cut' at the top of Lea Brook Road. When he arrived, he picked me up, and put me on top of the horse. (Didn't believe in that 'Diesel' stuff.) Considering I was about three at the time, and Grandad always used 'Heavy' horses, it was a long way up (or down), and I remember hanging on to the horse's collar.

"Lots more stuff about Grandad. Used to work for 'Caggy' Mitchell. Grandad was frequently called out by the police, if someone had gone into the cut. Seems he knew the currents and he knew where the body would be. I remember sitting on his knee, and by the time I was five I knew (in theory, at least) how to 'lock' a boat up or down. He was also a horse whisperer. I'll tell you sometime about the time he got it wrong . . .

"And we ain't even started on Uncle (Captain) Colin Whitehouse D.S.O. and Bar. Or the fact that when my other half, the Lovely Linda, and myself, did our family tree, a few years ago, we found that a couple of our ancestors knew each other, in the First World War.

"The photo is of the big guy Joseph Silwood – a boatman and legend in his own lifetime. This photo was took when I was about four years old, which means that it was about 1953 when Grandad would have been about 65 years old. As for the location, as best as I can remember it, if you stand in front of the 'Shrubbery' pub in Tipton and look over to your left hand side (where there are houses now) in those days, it was open fields. I seem to recall there were all sorts of games, and there was a fair.

"Going off on another tangent my great grandfather on the other side of the family was the first company secretary of Fellows, Morton and Clayton, the great canal carrying company. He was Alderman Ruben Farley JP. But that's another story as you may well already know!"

Barry and Grandad.

Life in Pump Street

Michael Relves of Links Road, **Penn** was born on 23 April 1942 at 10, Pump Street, **Ettingshall**, then part of **Bilston**, the middle child of three. His dad, Jesse, came from Rough Hills, **Parkfields**, whilst his Mom, Hilda, was born in Newport, Monmouthshire. She came to the Midlands in 1932 when she was fifteen, when her parents moved in search of work. At the time of Michael's birth, his family was "living with my Nanny May and my Step-Grandfather, James Hampton (Edward – Mom's father had passed away in February 1937) and my brother Stanley had already been on the scene for six years, hogging the limelight. Through our talks over the years I can judge he was already causing moments of blind panic for Mom and Dad, such as walking off and falling in the locks on the local canal off Ettingshall Road, needing to be rescued by the cottage owner alongside the locks and canal tow path.

"Number 10, Pump Street was one of a pair of houses with a central entry passage to the back yard and individual front doors. The back yard was complete with separate brewhouses and outside toilets and a separate coal house. Number 10, which was to be my home for a further eleven years, was situated near the end of Pump Street at its junction with Sweetbriar Road. All the houses in the street were the terraced type with shared back yards and I suppose ours was one of a pair of larger houses at each end of the terrace.

"The house had three bedrooms with no bathroom and a small cellar in the middle located under the stairs. There were two rooms downstairs, the front parlour and the back room serving as the living room and kitchen. This room was equipped with a cast iron 'Zebo' black-leaded grate which had a wooden

Stafford Road, Wolverhampton in the early 1900s. Thanks to Wolverhampton Archives and Local Studies.

surround and mantle shelf which I remember always seemed to have a red Chenille fringe fitted.

"This grate was the heart of the house providing heating and cooking facilities – an oven for baking and a hob to boil up kettles or saucepans. The only other means of boiling a kettle or a saucepan was a gas ring burner which I recall from my toddler days was always attached to a smelly rubber pipe, reeking of gas, in a half-perished state and always on the verge of falling apart. I wasn't to know it at the time but it really was quite unsafe.

"Each of the downstairs rooms had a central ceiling mounted gas light and upstairs the only means of lighting was by means of small dumpy candles called 'Night Lights', which were placed on a saucer. The other alternative was paraffin lamps. There was electricity supplied to the house and I was about nine years old before a power supply was finally installed. I think Mom and Dad had to pay for the supply to be connected.

"The general sleeping arrangements in the house were that Stanley had the smaller front bedroom, Nan and Jim in the other front bedroom and I shared the back bedroom with Mom and Dad in a cot alongside their bed. One of my earliest memories was of Mom and Dad cutting out and pasting animal pictures on the wall adjacent to me. I think they were from comics or similar and I'm sure that I must have been the youngest person to spot a Hippo or Rhino in darkest Ettingshall."

Wash Day Blues: "It's amazing how as a young child you gradually become aware of your surroundings and weekly events. Each Monday I would be placed into a high chair and taken to the brewhouse and although this was not attached to the house this would become the warmest room to be in, the fire having been lit early in the morning under the boiler tub.

"As a child I was fascinated by all the bits and pieces used in the process – the wooden dollies, podging sticks and the generous dollop of Rinso or Oxydol washing powder applied to the water. My particular favourite was the little linen bags called Dolly Blue which were put into the water and I think these were an additive to make sure the whites in the washing came out sparkling.

"The washing was then taken from the boiler and transferred to a zinc bath and carried outside to an old upright iron mangle with large wooden rollers and I always remember the wood on these rollers being bleached white. Each washing load was then manhandled through the rollers to remove the water and the washing could be pegged out on the line. The complete process would take up the whole of each Monday."

Hard Tough Days

Mr R. Mason of Oakfield Road, **Bilbrook**, **Wolverhampton** was born in 1928 and recalls "my Dad although a skilled tradesman was put out of work. We had a wonderful Indian doctor, a Doc Fozdar who brought me into this world, with no doubt a lot of others, at a princely cost of 7s 6d in old money, my Ma told me. It was a lot of money those days and he accepted 2/6d a week on the never never, Hospitals had to be paid for and it was the norm for docs to attend. He was a saint that man and he had a street named after him in Bilston (off Castlecroft Road) when he died in the 60s. I think he was loved by all as he stood by you in your illness (time of need) and helped your medical needs like a friend of the family!

"That was in Daisy Bank near Bradley. My Dad used to take me for walks after meeting me after infants school at Ladymoor, till my mother came back from a part time (for peanuts) job as a cleaner. They had five of us to rear, on nothing, two boys and three girls, which was at the lower size of families those days. We had oil lamps hanging from the ceiling for light; one toilet for three families out in a cold dark yard.

"There was a pub a few yards away. They called it 'Shuttees' I think because it was owned by a man called Shut. It had a large rough space in front of it, and every

Saturday night a butcher would be there selling what my mother called 'KAG MAG'. She would never buy off him because she believed a lot of it was condemned meat. The pubs closed at 10 pm and 9.30 pm, he would close his shop van and go in there for a drink. But he used to throw scatter, a handful of farthings into the crowd of kids, and tell them to tell their mothers that his farthings were as good as his meat! The rush for the 'money' was total war, no mercy shown. If you didn't get a farthing you could be sure you got black nails and fingers.

"We left there (Daisy Bank) for Chapel Street, Bilston, because my Grandma died and my Grandad was ill and needed help. That was eight of us now in a small terraced house, sharing a toilet outside with another two families of ten and nine, plus us made it twenty-seven using one toilet, which was outside

The back of 172 and 173, Hanley Street in the Summer Lane neighbourhood of Birmingham in the 1930s – emphasising the problems of bad housing faced by so many people in Birmingham and the Black Country.

and attached to the ashpit so when if somebody threw ashes in while you were on the 'throne' all the dust came onto you. Toilet paper was supplied by the *Express and Star*! There was no lights there, unless you took a candle. The baths were tin baths in front of the fire, but 'modern' gas lighting. My grandfather was an organist at St Mary's, Oxford Street for a while and later at the Methodist, Swan Bank . . .

"I went to Loxdale School up the road and I remember how poor the people were. We went to school and kids had no breakfast and used to pick apple cores out of the gutters and eat them, or part of an orange. Dinners for some were sugar and bread, or sauce and bread! We had what we called 'POBBIES', milk with bits of ordinary bread in it. We were lucky, my dad got a job at last in 1936 at the Singer Motor works at Small Heath, B'ham. He was on edge there because they 'STOPPED AND STARTED' ON A MINS NOTICE, as the sign said in the Manager's Office, no matter how long (and lucky) you had been there. We only saw him at weekends, after mid-day Saturday, because he left at six in the morning and didn't come back till 9 pm. One day in 1937 he told my mother that

The back of houses in Charles Street, Wolverhampton, perhaps 1950s. Thanks to Wolverhampton Archives and Local Studies.

there was a war going to come soon as work on cars was slowly being changed to making air-craft parts for 'Wellingtons'. She was shocked when he told her the firm wanted him to live near the works so he could spend more time there, and refused to go. In 1941 the houses round the works were bombed and we should have been killed.

"In 1938 we moved to Moseley Road, Bilston into a brand new council house in the 'country' then, and enjoyed a built in bath, electric lighting and a garden front and rear and toilet for ourselves and not half the street!"